The Countryman's Field Sports

The Countryman's Field Sports Bible

By The Outdoorsman

Mr. A. E. Marchant

The Countryman's Field Sports Bible

The Countryman's Field Sports Bible

Copyright: A. E. Marchant

Published: 12/09/2013

Publisher: H.Harman

The right of A.E.Marchant to be identified as author of this Work has been asserted by her in accordance with sections 77 and 78 of the Copyright, Designs and Patents Act 1988.

All rights reserved. No part of this publication may be reproduced, stored in retrieval system, copied in any form or by any means, electronic, mechanical, photocopying, recording or otherwise transmitted without written permission from the publisher. You must not circulate this book in any format.

The Countryman's Field Sports Bible

Table of Contents

THE COUNTRYMAN'S FIELD SPORTS BIBLE 1

By The Outdoorsman 1

Mr. A. E. MarchantThe Countryman's Field Sports Bible 1

Introduction 7

Ferreting: Getting started 8

Feeding 10

Ferrets in General 11

Ferret Breeding 14

Nets and Purse Net Settings 16

Setting the Nets 17

Ferreting with Dogs 18

Time of Year to go 19

The Hunt with Ferrets 21

Lay Ups 22

Dispatching the Rabbit 24

Gutting or Paunching and Skinning 25

The Countryman's Field Sports Bible

The Art of Snaring Rabbits 30

Setting the Snare 32

Long Netting with Ferrets etc 33

Using a Long Net at Night 36

Shooting Over Ferrets 38

Lamping at Night with a Shotgun 39

Time To Go 40

Lamping on your own 40

Lamping Skills 41

Shotguns For and Against 42

The Trusty 410 Shotgun 45

Shotgun Ballistics 46

The Barrel 46

CHOKINGS 47

Multi-Choke Guns 48

The Wad 49

Diameter of Spread 50

Recommended Shot Sizes for Game 51

Chokings for Game 54

The Countryman's Field Sports Bible

Rough Shooting 55

Pigeon Shooting over Decoys 55

Pigeon Shooting High Flying 55

Game Driven 55

Effective Range of Game Cartridges 56

Striking Velocity 58

Details of Shot Sizes 59

Relative Sizes of Shot 59

Forward Allowance 61

Weights of Game 64

British Game Shooting Seasons 65

Air Guns and Air Gun Shooting 66

Spring Powered Weapons 68

CO2 Gas Weapons 68

Pre-Charged Weapons 69

Gas Ram Air Rifles. 71

Pump up Weapons. 72

CAL .177 .20 .22 .25 73

Air Gun Ballistics 77

The Countryman's Field Sports Bible

Air Gun Ammunition	79
Sniping Shooting with Air Guns.	80
Crow Decoying	85
Crow and Magpie Decoying	86
RABBITS	89
Pigeon Decoying and Pigeon Shooting	91
RECONNAISANCE	93
Pigeon Decoying from a Hide and Equipment Needed	94
Pigeon Decoying – Crops	96
ROOST SHOOTING	97
Farm Buildings etc.	99
Clothing	100
SCOPES	101
Night Vision Scopes	103
Equipment in the Field	105

The Countryman's Field Sports Bible

Introduction

The Outdoorsman was born, works and remains in Sussex. He has practised the art of field craft for over forty years and this book is intended to help the novice and to some extent the more experienced. It is written mainly from personal experience and with personal bias, but hopefully will provide a good grounding for the uninitiated. Other material, such as ballistics have been drawn from technical articles which are widely available to all. The Outdoorsman and the rest of his team who produced this book, hope you find it informative and enjoyable to read. Good luck and good hunting.

The Outdoorsman.

The Countryman's Field Sports Bible

Ferreting: Getting started

Ferrets need a good dry home to come back to. Not too draughty, especially in the sleeping quarters. You can utilise a shop bought rabbit hutch for the purpose or indeed adapt it to have an open air run, which I prefer for a number of reasons. Ferrets like to play and keep active with a bit of space and they even sleep outside on warm days. A happy ferret will reward you better on hunting days. Perhaps provide them with a ball to play with or a hammock to sleep in, which can be made with a piece of sacking. The nest area or sleeping quarters should be filled with straw especially in the winter months. Ferrets always do their toilet in the same corner so having an open type of cage is easier for cleaning out i.e moving the cage frequently or hosing down the area. Ferrets rarely use the nest box as a toilet as they are generally very clean animals, but all ferrets smell and rabbits know it.

The Countryman's Field Sports Bible

Of course you will also need a hunting carry box. The box as shown in the photograph has two compartments. The reason being that when undoing the box they will all try to get out, so by having two compartments you can control them one at a time and work with the one you want more easily. I don't like ferret carry bags because if you fall or trip over onto the bag they are dead.

TIP: When working one ferret always have the other ferret boxed and away from the burrow as it will scratch and make unnecessary noise, but more of that later.

The Countryman's Field Sports Bible

Feeding

Ferrets should be fed twice a day, once in the morning and once in the evening. In the winter months when you are catching rabbits keep the liver, kidneys and heads; ferrets love the heads especially the brains. If not selling the rabbit, cut off the rib cage and use for food as this is not a cut unless making a stew for home use. In the spring/summer feed your ferrets on dog food which they love or one of the dry ferret mixes. Use a drip bottle on the side of the cage in case they run out of milk or water in the daytime. Try to get heavy bowls so the ferrets don't play with them and tip them over. You can treat them out of hunting season with a portion of liver from your local butcher at little cost. Your ferrets will look healthy and look after your sport if you look after them. It is also a good idea to put a few drops of cod liver oil in their food. If you have a rabbit that is not fit for the table, gut it and put the whole carcase in the cage.

The Countryman's Field Sports Bible

They enjoy eating everything except the bones and I think it makes them better hunters for this.

TIP: Never feed before going out hunting or let them eat whilst hunting.

Ferrets in General

The male ferret is called a Hob and the female a Jill. The hob ferret is not normally used for working because of its size and strength. It is impossible for the Hob to pass through the net on entry or exit so you are always lifting the net aside for access and resetting and this is very time consuming. Also because of its strength, a hob can hold onto a rabbit and kill underground, hence a layup. They can be used as a line ferret i.e. a cord is attached to its collar and put to ground to find a dead rabbit. You then dig down and follow the cord or gently pull on the line hoping the hob won't let go of the rabbit and retrieve it for you that way, known as liners. This is more a thing of the past as we now have electronic ferret finders, but more of that later. Hobs are best kept as pets really or for breeding. The Jill needs to be as small as possible for hunting purposes. Some people breed what is known as a greyhound, very small indeed and very good workers. When buying your ferrets young try to see both parents as this will give you a good idea of its eventual size. Also buy from good working stock. Ferrets come in various different types, albinos are white with pink eyes.

The Countryman's Field Sports Bible

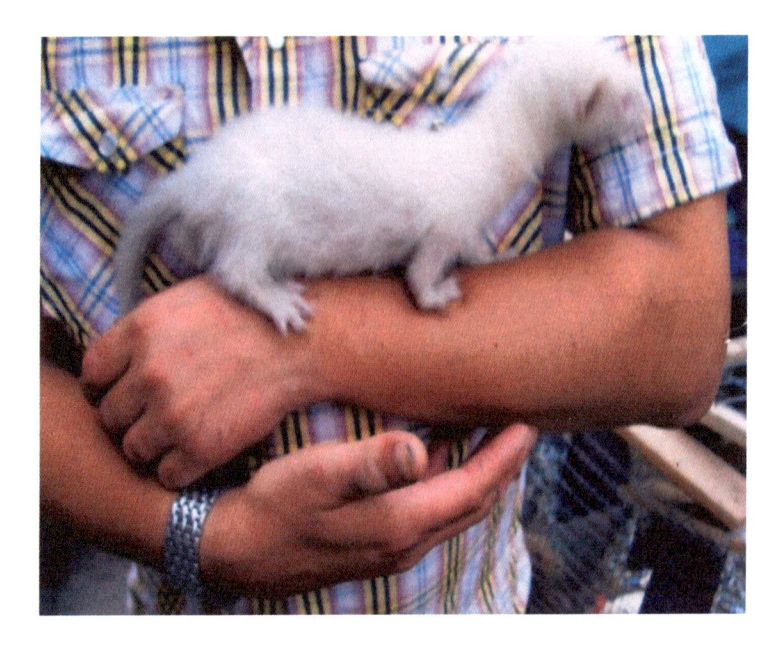

Albinos are my favourite as they seem to work more quickly than the polecat and show up better against the undergrowth. Polecats can vary in colour by mainly cross breeding with albinos. A true polecat has distinct colours of black, brown and cream as shown in the next photograph.

The Countryman's Field Sports Bible

Ferrets like a walk sometimes and for this you will need a ferret harness or collar and lead.

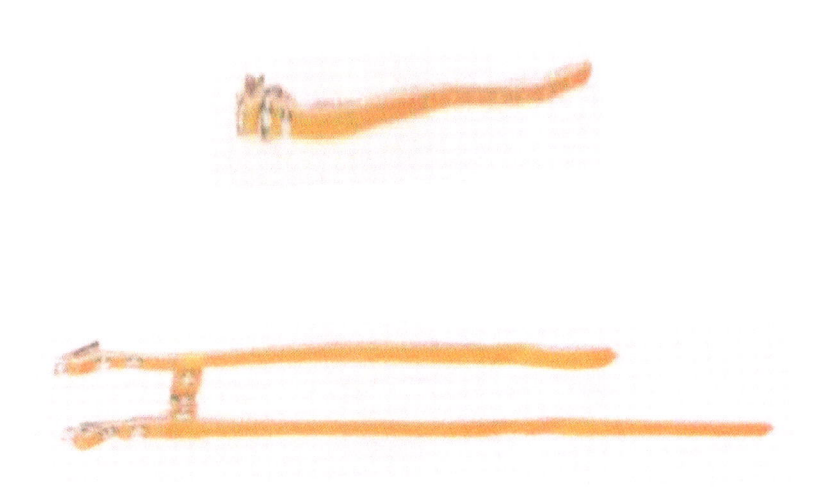

Some people like to have ferrets as pets only, so the harness or collar is very useful. Handle your ferrets as much as possible when they are young so they get used to you. They can be very playful and interesting animals and a lot of fun. Keep them clean at all times, changing their bedding regularly and cleaning out their hutch is very important if you want healthy ferrets. If you see any

signs of tics, use a cotton bud dipped in methylated spirit, as this will release the tic from the ferret. If you try to pull the tic out without doing

The Countryman's Field Sports Bible

this the head of the tic will remain in the skin and could possibly become septic.

TIP: Tics are normally around sheep but ferrets can pick them up anywhere, so can your dog or cat for that matter. A tic buries its head into the animal and has barbs to prevent it from being pulled out. The part of the tic showing will be white if it hasn't been there very long otherwise it will be a blue/black colour as it feeds on the blood. Check your ferrets regularly for this especially around the ears. If you have any problems with this consult your vet. I would not advise a muzzle when hunting as they can get caught up on roots underground and if you have a ferret that bites you it is because you haven't handled it enough. A ferret should have the right to defend itself underground. In the past some inhumane people used to practice the removal of the fang teeth so the ferret could not kill underground. This to me is a disgusting act that should never be followed.

Ferret Breeding

Breeding ferrets is not that difficult, but as with all animals there are do's and don'ts. The ferret needs to be at least one year old, hob or jill. Try to select the smallest hob and jill from good working stock, this way you have more chance of having a small greyhound - workers ideal for hunting. The adult jill comes into season in the spring and you will notice the genital area is swollen and pink in colour with a slight discharge, and

The Countryman's Field Sports Bible

this is quite normal. Now is the time to put the hob with her for mating. Mating can last a day or so with the hob biting the jill, holding on and not letting her go. They will make a lot of noise as if in pain and blood may appear from the jills neck but do not be alarmed or disturb the pair as this is quite normal.

After mating remove the hob and leave the jill on her own in the hutch. The hob now serves no other purpose as the jill will bring the kits up when born. If breeding two jills at the same time it is best to have them in separate hutches. I have known breeding jills to to eat the other jills kits if kept together. You will notice the milk teats forming as time goes by and an increase in weight. The gestation period is between thirty eight and forty four days. Make sure there is plenty of hay in the nesting compartment as the jill will make a nice cosy nest. Do not clean out or disturb the nest and keep it dry. When the kits are born leave them well alone, do not touch or handle them. She may give birth to between four and eight and eat some, maybe the weak ones, or she knows that she will not have sufficient milk to feed them all, but that is nature for you. The kits are born hairless with their eyes closed and are reared by the mother. Sometimes when the jill leaves the nest to feed the kits may hang on to her teats, do not interfere as the jill will take them back to her nest. The kits eyes will open between twenty and thirty days and they can start to be fed from a shallow bowl, bread and milk is ok, then try mashed soft dog food, and they also like raw egg. You can handle them around this time although they may like to nip with their milk teeth. When they are taking solids and active and are no longer dependant on the jill they must be kept warm and dry. The jill may change colour and lose weight but will soon return to normal.

The Countryman's Field Sports Bible

Nets and Purse Net Settings

The nets for ferreting are called purse or flop nets. They can be made of nylon or hemp but I prefer the nylon type, the difference being they are cheaper, don't rot in wet weather and in my opinion are easier to work with. I like to use a four foot net rather that a three foot. You will need pegs for the nets made of hazel cut from a hedgerow. The pegs should be three or four inches long with a hole drilled through the side at the top to attach the net. Push the loose cord through the hole and loop it around itself, this way the peg cannot come off. (See photograph)

The Countryman's Field Sports Bible

Setting the Nets

When setting a net, first quietly remove twigs, leaves and other debris from around the hole, because if the net catches on these it will not draw closed. Push the peg in at the top about six inches up from the hole. This is to provide a split second grab action as the rabbit hits the net and causes it to close; remember to keep the top ring clear to draw.

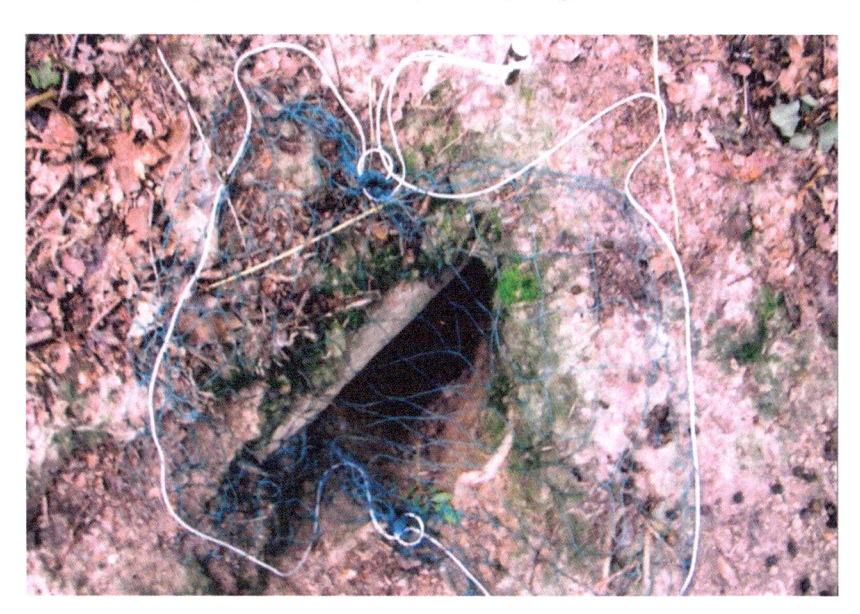

You may need fifty to a hundred nets depending on your ground and your warren/bury sizes. When picking up your nets hold the bottom ring then the top ring and pull the top ring to the peg. Pull the peg out and let the net dangle by the bottom ring. Roll the net around your hand from the bottom ring to the peg. You will need a small net bag or large pockets.

The Countryman's Field Sports Bible

Ferreting with Dogs

Well now you are all set up to go ferreting; you have your ferrets, nets and carry box. So what about a dog? Ferreting without a dog is called blind ferreting, the reason being that without a dog you don't know for sure if the rabbits are at home in the warren. Very time wasting setting all those nets for no result. Jack Russell or terrier type dogs are the best although any dog with a good nose can be trained to hunt with you, and they love it.

Training a dog to mark for you means they will tell you if there are rabbits at home. Let the dog sniff the holes and watch carefully for any signs of

The Countryman's Field Sports Bible

marking. Dogs vary in how they mark, some will stand in front of the hole very still, others may stand and shiver; it is for you to recognise your dogs' way of signing. Once you have confidence in your dog always go by it. You may have to go a few times with the dog for it to learn what's going on but once the dog knows and the rabbits start hitting the net, you're there. You will find your dog an invaluable asset. Keep the dog away from the holes once the ferrets go to work, generally in the middle of the warren; if the rabbits see you or the dog they may not bolt. They would rather face the ferret and of course this may lead to as lay up - very time consuming and hard work.

Time of Year to go

The time of year to go ferreting is in the winter. Years ago they used to say when there is an 'R' in the month, but that I believe is when we used to have proper winters. The seasons seem to have changed now, so I go depending on the year, say November till the end of February. You will see when to stop ferreting as you will catch pregnant or milky does and you don't want a lay up i.e. the ferret kills the rabbit or eats the young ones and then goes to sleep.

Whatever the weather you can ferret if you have suitable clothing to wear. In the rain a military breathable jacket and trousers will keep you dry. Bearing in mind you will be on your knees when setting the nets I would recommend this type of clothing. Ferreting in the rain has some advantages. Rabbits like to stay as dry as possible, as you do, so if you think about it maybe more rabbits will go to ground to stay dry,

The Countryman's Field Sports Bible

something I learned years ago. I have had some of my best ferreting in the rain. Keep ferrets as dry as possible, as they do not like to get wet either.

Hunting in the snow was always my favourite. The atmosphere of the day was so exciting, the silence and the chill of the air makes the day. In the snow you will see what has happened; footprints, rabbit droppings, urine patches and the scent for the dog and ferrets is a lot better and lasts longer in cold weather. If you know your warrens well, don't forget the small bolt holes as the rabbits will allow these to cover over with snow and will not use them unless in an emergency. As a rule, only the main holes will be used in the snow.

Ferreting in strong winds is not always the best time to go. The rabbits do not bolt so well, maybe they smell you and the dog, I don't know, but high winds were not my favourite time. You cannot hear what is going on underground, which is very important sometimes, but I still caught rabbits! So to summarise; winter time, a cold dry morning and frost is the best, the ground is hard and easier to walk, the rabbits seem to get cold and go to ground more and bolt out a lot better - really hitting the nets. You can hear well what is going on underground, very much like thunder under your feet.

The Countryman's Field Sports Bible

The Hunt with Ferrets

When starting the hunt, first find the warren/earth, (or in the south called a burry) and set the purse nets as described earlier in the book. Keep as quiet as possible when doing this, very important, as the rabbits will stay and rather face the ferrets instead of bolting out. You can enter the ferret by lifting the net or if you have a small jill pass her through the net. Sometimes if you have no dog to tell you if the quarry is at home, the ferret will shake or its tail will expand, a good sign of an experienced ferret. Once the ferret has entered the hole, try to keep it as near as possible to the middle of the burry, so bolting rabbits will not see you and attempt to go back to ground. Always keep a few spare nets in your pocket because when the first rabbit hits the net you may have more coming up behind. Hold the rabbit in the net and put your foot over the hole. Despatch the rabbit in the net and reset another net straight away.

Do not automatically think a big warren or earth is very good, they can be very time wasting. I have had six rabbits from a single hole, very quickly, as it sometimes happens. You will soon get to know your ground. Look for the secret pop up holes which are sometimes covered by a clump of grass etc, away from the earth; this is their natural escape route. When the ferret is working you will hear the ground thunder as the bolting rabbit tries to escape. Be ready for action.

You will soon know when to move on and when to pick up the nets. The ferrets will not stay to ground and the experienced will move off to find another burry. Very exciting to watch, and make ready for the next. When I said a very big warren is not so easy to work with, try the long net around the burry. This will work well for you as explained later in the book. I used to know some very big warrens by lakes. Too big to flop net,

The Countryman's Field Sports Bible

so I used the long nets to start from the water's edge and ringed it right round the warren. Stay well inside the long net and let the ferrets work on their own. When a rabbit hits the net, despatch in the net and leave it alone, then wait for the next one. I have seen rabbits swim across a lake, rather than hit the net, with the dog swimming behind in hot pursuit but the rabbit always swam faster. Who said rabbits couldn't swim!

Lay Ups

If you get a layup this means the ferret has either killed underground or got stuck behind another rabbit. One will never know what happens underground. If this happens try to call the ferret by squeaking or stamp your feet on the ground. On a small burry I would block all the holes and come back the next day to uncover the holes and maybe your ferret will come out. An electronic ferret locater would make a good part of your kit. The modern ones have come a long way and I recommend the use of them. Many more rabbits will be added to the bag and you will know more of what is going on underground.

A folding spade is a must to take with you; one of the military types is ideal and has more uses than you think. I have ferreted on beach stones in the south where most of the burries are very shallow. In a layup the spade was invaluable.

Over the years working with ferrets sometimes you get a surprize visitor in a burry. I have had squirrels, stoats, weasels, fox and mink bolt. None of these seem to like the ferret but I have known my ferrets to be killed underground by foxes and badgers, although this is a relatively rare experience. Sometimes other animals will use a rabbit burry in an

The Countryman's Field Sports Bible

emergency to hide up from danger and stay underground waiting until dark to go to safety. Living in the south we have very sandy soil with a lot of chestnut woods, loved by the rabbits because it is easy digging for them to start new burries etc., and the soil is very dry which they appreciate. I really like to work these woods, it is so much easier to net up than thick hedgerows, but these must be worked as well to keep the land owner happy, without him you would have no sport.

If you have very thick hedges etc, either set the long net as explained or clear with a machete around the holes. Do not do this on the same day as the hunt as you will make too much noise and get problems, i.e. layups. If you clear these buries of thick undergrowth etc a week or so before you hunt the rabbits will get used to the change very quickly and make the setting of nets much easier. Worth the effort and very rewarding for the future. Do not cut into the hedges, only make netting of the holes easier for yourself or you may upset the land owner. Damage by you must be less than the rabbits.

TIP: If the ferret has killed underground, for example reappears blood stained, use a long bramble to go down the hole and turn it at the same time. Withdraw the bramble and look for fur on the thorns, this will show how far down it is and will maybe indicate if it is worth digging to retrieve the dead rabbit.

The Countryman's Field Sports Bible

Dispatching the Rabbit

This is something that is not often read about or lived by townies etc., or by 'do gooders' i.e. Anti-blood sport. Always dispatch humanely and cleanly. Very important to yourself and the rabbit, or for that matter any living animal or fish on earth. I have no time for any person who kills inhumanely and take country sport as fun. This gives field sports a very bad name and ruins the future of the countryside. I prefer to dispatch the rabbit in the net, it is quick, easy and once killed you can leave it in the there and reset another net quickly. You can untangle the rabbits from the nets when you have finished working the burry. This also applies to working a long net.

Hold the rabbit around the back of the neck in the left hand, and with the palm of the right hand under its chin, push upward to break its neck. Very quick and humane.

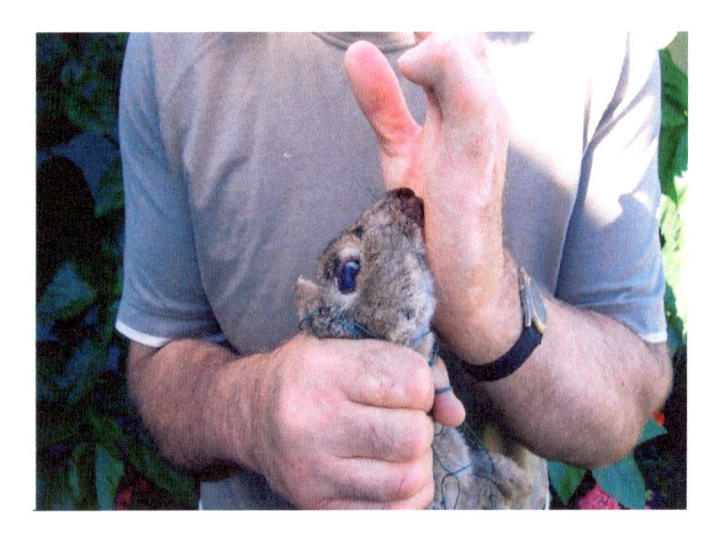

The Countryman's Field Sports Bible

You will not find killing out of the net very easy because the back legs will kick you hard and inflict some nasty scratches on your hands. Best leave the rabbit in the net as this will alleviate the problem. If you must dispatch the rabbit out of the net then always hold the rabbit by its back legs so it cannot kick or scratch you. To despatch this way, hold the rabbit by its back legs with your right hand, then with the left hand around its neck pull over your leg hard and slightly twist. All over and very quick. See photograph.

Gutting or Paunching and Skinning

Now we have our rabbits we have to gut, or 'paunch' them.

The Countryman's Field Sports Bible

Firstly I like to let the rabbit cool off a little. Before you start to paunch, you must make the rabbit urinate. This is because if the bladder is burst or cut in the paunching process it will taint the flesh.

This act is very easy to do, simply hold the rabbit's back legs downward and put slight pressure on the gut, about four inches from its tail and the urine will be expelled. Once you have done this you may paunch or gut. See photograph.

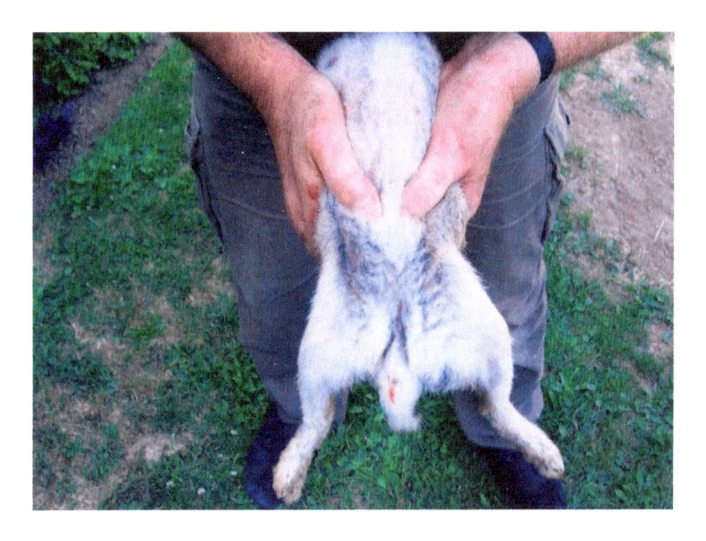

There are many ways to paunch. You will need a small knife, one of the French Opinel knives are ideal as they lock and are made of carbon steel. They have a good edge and are very good value. They are numbered according to size but I think a number 5 or 6 is very useful for this purpose. Always keep it sharp. There are diamond sharpeners on the market; one of the best is made by buck of America with a diamond edge you could shave with. After a good sharpening a knife is a good safe tool to use and work with.

First hold the rabbit head downwards, the reason for this is that the gut will fall forwards. Enter the knife between the back legs and cut up to the rib cage. Do not use a lot of the blade, only the tip otherwise you will cut

The Countryman's Field Sports Bible

into the gut and make a very messy job of it. Something you will not do again. Once you have done this I prefer to hold the rabbit by its head and back legs and swing it sideways, the gut should then fly out, no messy hands etc. I do remember seeing this done many years ago in an old American book and I adapted this technique for its easy use.

Always check the liver, kidneys and eyes and the general condition of the rabbit. The liver should be a nice brown colour with no orange rings or spots, or growths for that matter, as this could indicate cancer etc.

The kidneys should be half covered in vat, a very good sign of a healthy rabbit. The eyes should be sparkling and clear with no sign of Myxomatosis. If in doubt, disregard for the table and give to the ferret, or disregard altogether. Keep the liver and kidneys as they are a very useful food source and dispose of the rest in the field. Foxes etc. will soon clear it up so why take it home?

You will probably skin your rabbits at home, not always the case, but if you do you will have to carry them. I prefer to cross leg them and carry on a pole. Simply cut through one back leg and push the other through the slot. Very easy to do.

The Countryman's Field Sports Bible

Skinning the rabbit: People have different ideas, my way is to snap both back and front lags half way up and cut off, leaving the head on at this time. Where you have made the cut in the belly to gut

start to pull the skin apart sideways. Pull the skin over the back legs. When this is done hold the back legs with one hand and pull down to the head. Then cut the head off. Very simple to do.

The Countryman's Field Sports Bible

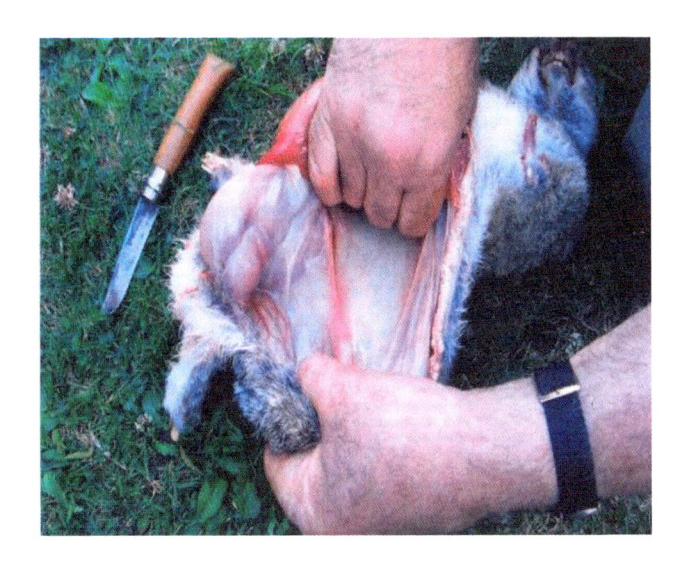

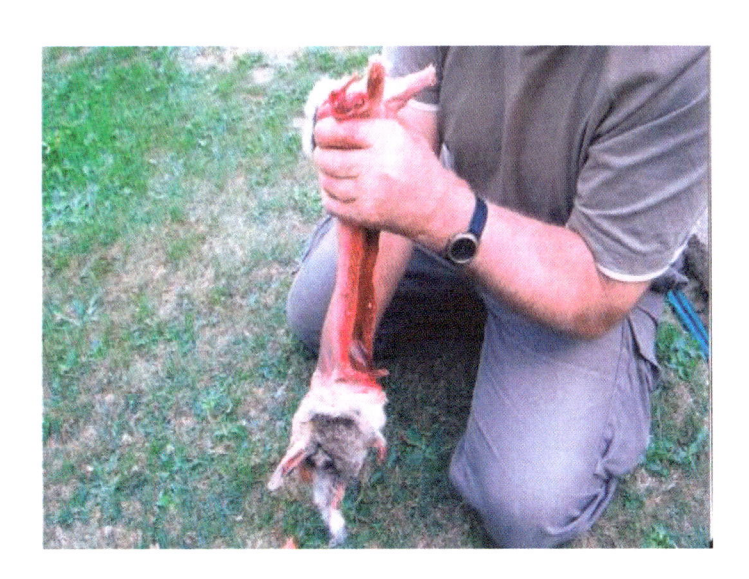

The Countryman's Field Sports Bible

The tail normally stays put, so cut down either side and pull the tail out, this will normally remove a small part of the bowel as well.

Once skinned remove the kidneys and the lungs and wash thoroughly. If the rabbit is for the table cut it into joints and leave in salt water overnight. This will remove a layer of skin and make the meat much better for cooking.

The Art of Snaring Rabbits

The snaring of rabbits can be a very effective way to control them, for example, when you cannot ferret in the spring or summertime or when the rabbit warren is not on your ground.

Rabbits may feed on your ground but come from somewhere else i.e. railway embankments or ground where permission to hunt cannot be obtained. Snares should be checked twice a day; in the morning and just before dark, to dispatch any live rabbits and to reset any unset or knocked over snares. You will need 50 or more to work with, depending on your ground. Pegs will be required, made of hazel is best, about as thick as your thumb and 6 inches long. Cut a nice point at one end and drill a hole through the side at the other end to put the cord through. Loop the cord over the snare so there is no way the peg can come off.

The Countryman's Field Sports Bible

You will also need for each snare a pricker stick to hold the snare in position. Again made from hazel about the size of a biro pen, cut a point at one end and a slit down about half an inch at the other end.

Snares are set in the rabbit runs mainly in open fields. These are like rabbit roadways and can easily be seen. Sometimes the snares can be set at hedgerows or fences where the rabbits regularly come through or under.

The Countryman's Field Sports Bible

Setting the Snare

You now have your snares attached to the pegs and your pricker sticks to hand, so now to set the snare. Push or hammer the peg into the ground to the side of the run, then put your fist in the snare and pull tight, this is about the size of the hole in the snare. Bend the wire slightly to stop the snare springing open, then set the snare using the pricker stick over the rabbit run as high as your hand from the ground. Use the pricker stick to hold the snare in position, with the wire pushed into the slit.

Snares can be set in the same way at fences or hedgerows where the rabbits regularly run. In the long evenings of summer it is possible to catch rabbits whilst being there. It pays to walk round every hour or so to check on your work. Be very careful where you use snares. Check there are no sheep or domestic cats in the area, as you do not want to upset the land or pet owner. One more reason to check snares regularly.

The Countryman's Field Sports Bible

TIP: Before use of new snares hang up to weather and take away any unnatural scent. Or bury in the ground for a short while.

Long Netting with Ferrets etc

Sometimes a long net when ferreting can be very useful, especially when cover is too thick to set purse nets or the bury or warren is too big to net. Long nets usually come in lengths of 25 yards to 100 yards. I advocate the 100 yard net for most uses. When you purchase your net it will not come with sticks, so cut some hazel about two and a half feet long and about as thick as your thumb. You will need a stick about every 10 yards, so cut ten for 100 yard net.

A 100 yard net has 50 yards of spare netting loose running. It is important to spread the net evenly between the sticks, which will allow bagging. If the net is too tight the rabbits will bounce off it.

Long nets have countless uses when used in ferreting situations where purse netting would prove too time consuming and labour intensive. Imagine a thick hedge, say especially blackthorn; impossible to enter to set purse nets and the perfect scenario for the use of long nets.

You should set your long net at right angles to the hedge on both sides if possible, with two small nets crossing the sides. This will stop the rabbits running sideways along the hedge, as they may do this rather than running out into the open field.

The Countryman's Field Sports Bible

Having the long nets as far out as possible enables the rabbits to get well clear of the warren or burry. Stand against the hedge, not in front of the net otherwise they will see you and run back to the warren and will not bolt out again, leading to a possible kill underground; not good as you may have to wait sometime before you get your ferrets back. I like to set purse nets on bolt holes if accessible from the hedge as they will try to use them. If there are two people, stand one each side of the hedge, so any rabbits bolting away from the perceived danger area will hit the net at full speed and become tangled. Kill the rabbits in the net and leave until later.

The nets do not have to be set very high off the ground. My pegs are only about two and a half feet long and when pushed in leave the net standing about 20 inches off the ground. The most important thing is to have plenty of loose netting between the pegs. If you have the net too tight like a tennis net the rabbits will bounce off and will not tangle in it. I like my long net pegs to be made from hazel which I may have explained. The nets top and bottom line should be held by a couple of half hitches in the traditional method of setting.

The Countryman's Field Sports Bible

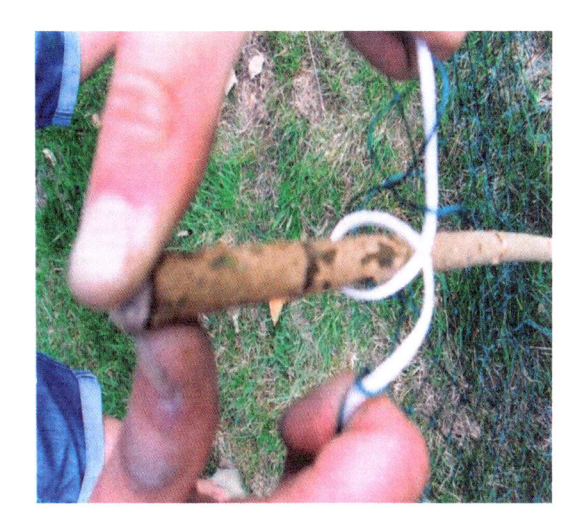

When a warren or bury is too big on open ground, ring the long net around. You can make any shape you like but keep ten paces between the pegs.

The Countryman's Field Sports Bible

It is important to stand in the middle of the warren and let the rabbits hit the net, if not they will bolt back. You will be amazed at the extra time you can save and the extra rabbits you can catch with the careful positioning of a long net. When picking up the net make sure to hold the spare netting i.e. the bag between pegs. Collect up the net by winding it between your thumb and over your elbow. When collected up use the peg cords to tie the net together. Collected this way, the net will be easy to reset next time.

TIP: Never wear clothing with buttons as they always catch on the net.

Using a Long Net at Night

It takes practice in the day time to set a long net at night. Try and get a good reliable hunting mate to set and reset the net with you, so that you know how to work together in silence. Don't forget to wear clothing without buttons.

When you can set the net with ease in the day it is time for night setting. Firstly know where to set it; know your ground and study it. The rabbits will come out to feed into the field, well out from the warren. Keep very quiet and if you smoke, don't. Very important. Keep downwind and set the net where you know the rabbits will bolt back to the warren. In most cases this will be back to the hedgerow to reach home. The net should be placed about 4 to 10 feet from the hedgerow.

The Countryman's Field Sports Bible

Once the net is set, one man will stay behind the net holding the top line in his fingers using both hands. By doing this he will know which way the rabbit has hit the net. The other person will then walk from the end of the net with a long length of cord, out around the field, as far as possible out from the net.

You should walk as far as possible out into the field and finish up at the other end of the net. The reason being, that the rabbits will not cross the cord when it touches them and hopefully they will run back to the warren and hit the net. As I said before, the rabbits should be killed in the net. Feel for the next rabbit with your fingers on the top line of the net. Sometimes you will have many rabbits hit the net at the same time; do not get excited and remain as silent as possible. When despatching rabbits at night, leave them lying upside down, as you will see their white bellies glowing in the dark, thus making them easier to find.

TIP: For good results always choose a dark night. i.e. no moon, and with a wind to hide any slight sound you may make. Collect up nets as described in ferreting with long nets.

The Countryman's Field Sports Bible

Shooting Over Ferrets

Shooting over ferrets can offer great sport, and in certain circumstances, a very good way of rabbit clearance. For example, when the cover is too thick to enter to net up, or maybe a large area of bramble in which it is almost impossible to work nets. But of course there are a few things to adhere to.

If using a trained dog, let the dog work in the thick cover at the same time the ferrets are at work, as very often the dog will catch rabbits in this way. But most importantly, always know where the dog is at all times.

Ferrets are best left to their own devices really, and a good ferret will work a thicket alone, entering the burry where it chooses. If the ferret wanders away a little try squeaking, they normally come to a squeak. It is a good idea to squeak when feeding them to teach them to come to call. It is important, if two people are shooting, to stand, if possible, in the middle of the burry, and stand back to back for safety reasons. This will also to cover the burry for all round shooting.

If possible let the rabbits run well out from the burry before taking a shot, although not always possible as sometimes they may re-enter the burry. This may cause a lay up, which can be time consuming and very frustrating. Also the noise of the gun may do this. Always keep noise to a minimum. The trusty .410 shotgun is more suited as it is quick to handle and obviously less noisy and really you cannot beat the .410 for shooting over burries. If shooting over a hedge line, with two people shooting, have one gun either side. Always stand face to face or back to back then you will always know where to shoot in confidence. For this type of shooting,

The Countryman's Field Sports Bible

in thick cover, it is another reason to prefer albino ferrets; they are easier to see than polecats.

Shooting over ferrets in certain circumstances can be very rewarding. But remember rabbits shot with a shotgun are not so good for the table, or so easy to sell to the butcher or game dealer. In my experience it is best to leave the gun at home and net up as much as possible. It is far more rewarding in the long run.

Lamping at Night with a Shotgun

Lamping at night can be very rewarding for good rabbit control and good sport with a shotgun. You will need a good lamper to work with you, as part of the team. Someone who will not lamp out of your range and knows your method of working.

In my early years of lamping there was not the choice of lamps and batteries that are available now. All we had was a large car battery carried on our back or on a trolley with a car headlamp, which were very heavy to carry and spillage of battery acid was common. A lot of good lamping kits are on the market now. For shotgun shooting, use dry type batteries as they will not spill and be a lot lighter to carry.

The lamp you will need should be of the hand held type with a beam of range 100 to 200 yards. Obviously you will not be shooting at this range but you will need this type of power when a red filter is in place as it vastly cuts the range down. Many lampers use red filters, but a change of colour can be advantageous. You can buy green, amber and blue. This is an important change especially if you often shoot over the same ground.

The Countryman's Field Sports Bible

Your quarry will sometimes get lamp shy and relate this to danger very quickly. Try to buy a lamp with a silent switch action, not all lamps have this. Rabbits will hear the switch on and off at quite a range.

For the type of battery kit to match your lamp, I recommend a 12 volt, 7.5 amp. This size of battery is an ideal size to carry and not too heavy. It should last, depending on your lamp size about 1 ½ to 2 hours. It is better to buy two batteries of this size if you require longer lamping hours than one big one, which can be very heavy and cumbersome to carry.

Time To Go

The best nights to go lamping are mainly due to the weather. Try to avoid moonlit nights; not ideal as the quarry will see you as well. Also no wind is not ideal, a light breeze will help to drown out your noise underfoot etc. A perfect night to go is with no moon and a breath of wind, do not worry about rain too much either. I have had some good nights lamping in the rain.

Lamping on your own

You can purchase shotgun lamping kits that work very well, but I have never really liked the idea for safety reasons, as you never know what can happen to you at night when you are on your own, I once knew of a man who was a very experienced person in this field, but had a nasty accident. He broke his leg while out, and in the days of no mobile phones was not able to call for assistance. He could not get back to the farm house or for that matter move at all and it was a very cold and rainy night. His wife did not know where he was and he had acres of land on different shoots. When he did not come home she raised the alarm, many hours later the

The Countryman's Field Sports Bible

next day they found him on one of his shoots nearly dead from the cold and the elements of the winter time. He spent a time in hospital. This is just one reason I do not recommend lamping on your own, very dangerous even for the professionals.

Lamping Skills

When lamping, if possible keep to the hedges and scan the lamp down and then out to the field. Do not lamp out of range.

Rabbits eyes will show up red at night. Fox eyes will show up a white/yellow. I have on occasions lamped woodcock feeding, their eyes also show red. If you are not sure of your target don't shoot. Keep side by side of each other when lamping for safety reasons, and keep as quiet as you can. Do not smoke and if possible keep the wind in your face, although this is not always possible.

It is a good idea to carry some type of torch with you for local light situations, i.e. checking your barrels are clear of any obstructions such as mud or snow, a very important thing to do if you do not want a burst barrel. This is very dangerous and I have witnessed such incidents.

If putting dead rabbits on the ground for any reason place them belly up, that way their white fur will show, much easier to see them at night whilst gutting etc. You will learn a lot about lamping for yourself; no shoot is the same as you will soon find out. Know your ground well, do reconnaissance in the day time and look out for ditches or other hazards. Try to pick a way around the shoot.

The Countryman's Field Sports Bible

Shotguns For and Against

Obviously one could write a complete book on shotguns, so in this chapter I will cover the basic pros and cons, in the first instance - gun types.

THE SIDE BY SIDE

I suppose the vast majority of people, shooters or otherwise, recognise the side by side as the traditional shotgun. Of course for over one hundred years and more, and up to this day, it has a strong traditional following. The top quality English gun makers tend to lend themselves to the world's best side by side game guns.

THE PROS:

1. Lighter to carry around the shoot for long periods.
2. Will carry more comfortably over your arm and also because of the smaller gape opening at the breach, will not keep hitting your legs as does the over and under.
3. Better for hide shooting i.e. pigeon decoying, sitting down to reload again, less room required, less gape on opening.
4. Most have auto safety catches, a must in rough shooting, in my opinion.
5. Cheaper to buy generally, especially in pre-owned guns.
6. Handles well with good pointability.

THE CONS:

The Countryman's Field Sports Bible

1. More recoil.
2. Most have double triggers. (Although very fast firing with practice).
3. Not often multi choked.
4. More heat distortion along sight plane. (Fast shooting clays)
5. Shooters with short or thick fingers may suffer from bruised second finger from the trigger guard.

Personally I use and have shot for many years with a 12 bore side by side, for rough and game shooting and also for clay pigeon. As you can see in the pros and cons there are a few points to bring to mind which I would like to enhance on. All side by sides are lighter than the under and over, around 6lbs. so recoil will be more, but for rough or game shooting this is not really a problem with good gun stance.

For clay pigeon there are a few makes that offer a heavier gun; multi choked with single select trigger with pistol grip and raised rib to eradicate heat haze. As for handling and pointability I personally believe they are more superior than the over and under. I don't think most people give the side by side a chance, mainly because of most having double triggers, but may I say with practice double triggers can be fired faster than single trigger counterparts.

Don't forget the famous shot Percy Stanbury, always shot clays with full choke using a side by side - unbeatable in his day. But as I have said, beware if short fingered as bruising will occur; if it does, the pistol grip stock with single trigger is a must.

As for value, £200 - £400 can purchase a good pre-owned gun, probably Spanish origin and made through the 60s to middle 80s for the U.K.

market. 28" barrels are mainly found as standard, the ideal length for all shooting in my opinion.

Clay guns are very well engineered to withstand many thousands of shots. Much heavier than the side by side to alleviate some recoil for continuous shooting, and much more comfortable to use. Many are also multi-choked for any type of shooting discipline; clays - short range skeet to long range sporting clays, or wildfowling or pigeon shooting. The multi-choke can come in to its own, a gun for all seasons.

THE PROS

1. Less recoil
2. Large grip bore end (no heat exchange from barrels to hands)
3. Single sight plane (note downfall for the inexperienced shot, tends to rifle shoot instead of keeping both eyes open for eye to hand co-ordination)
4. Most single select triggers.
5. Most multi-choked.
6. Strong construction.

THE CONS

1. Heavy to carry in the field all day.
2. More expensive.
3. Most do not have multi-safe.
4. More troublesome with ejectors.
5. When carried over arm tends to hit legs with the barrels.
6. Not so easy to re-load in hides, more gape to load bottom barrel, especially when sitting down.

As you will see the basic differences are for you to choose from. Always buy a gun that fits you well i.e. length of stock is very important. Note a simple test, put your finger on the trigger and lay the stock into your

The Countryman's Field Sports Bible

forearm, if there is a gap, the stock is too short. Too long, if you cannot place good trigger positioning. Also for gun fit, aim into a mirror; by your own eye you will then see any misalignment.

The Trusty 410 Shotgun

The .410 shotgun is an ideal gun to shoot rabbits with as it is light to carry all day and not an overkill gun. Very useful for shooting over burries. A lot of .410 guns were made in Spain and Belgium, and were very popular in the British market. Most of these were the fold in half type, and very popular with poachers because they could be carried under the coat on Sunday morning walks. Useful for obtaining your dinner as you made your way to Church. You will find quite a few of these guns with cut out stocks to make them even lighter to carry and use. A lot of people liked to customise these guns in this way.

Webley and Scott made a very nice .410 bolt action gun for his type of sport and El-Chimbo of Spain made many types of double hammer guns, most of which were of the fold down type. Beware of chamber sizes in .410 guns, some are only 2" chambers, most are 2 ½" long, but the magnum has 3" chamber; a very useful cartridge for this type of work. Make sure you use the correct length of cartridge for your gun, as some guns will accept a longer cartridge than proofed for. This is very important, so if in doubt consult your gun smith for advice.

Shot size for rabbits would be size 6, a good all round size of shot for this type of work and general shooting.

The Countryman's Field Sports Bible

Shotgun Ballistics

Understanding shotgun ballistics is a very important part of successful shot gunning. Whether it be for game or clay shooting, cartridge types and loads, plastic or fibre wads and shot sizes, all are important factors for the right combination to shoot your chosen quarry successfully.

The Barrel

Firstly the length of barrel forms no justification to range or killing power. Whether you have a 25" or 32" barrel the range and ft.lbs of energy are the same with modern day cartridges. This however was not true years ago when using black powder shotguns. Because of the slow rate of burn one needed a longer barrel to enable maximum velocity. In a shorter barrel the shot charge would have left the muzzle before maximum velocity was achieved.

The above was also a fact with earlier nitro cartridges in their infancy, but of course barrel length is still important to the shooter in regard to the discipline you are shooting. The 25" barrel is mainly used for quick pointability i.e. walked up game shooting or fast birds driven over a ride etc. But their downfall is that on crossing birds or high driven shots they lack the follow through for lead on the target and become twitchy. The most common of barrel lengths is of course the 28". It handles very well in most shooting situations and also suits Mr Average build and stance. Above 28", the 30" to 32" are more suited to long slow crossing birds and

The Countryman's Field Sports Bible

high driven shots and even down the line clay shots. It is surprising that 2" to 4" extra makes a more stable follow through or maintained lead way of shooting, but on saying this, the shooter must be of, in my opinion, above average build and stance to get the gun moving correctly on the target.

CHOKINGS

Chokings determine the diameter of the shot pattern at given ranges and are the most important part of shotgun ballistics. The last 2" of the muzzle is where the choking lays. Choking is a reduction in the diameter of the bore, for example; the less the reduction the greater the diameter the shot pattern at a given range. The more reduction in the bore the smaller the diameter of the shot pattern at a given range. But before we elaborate on this, one must first ascertain what choke our gun is bored to, especially if bought second hand. To find this, look on the underside of the barrels just in front of the bites you will normally notice stars. These indicate the chokings.

Chokings

1. * full
2. ** ¾
3. *** ½
4. **** ¼

Of course if the gun has been bored out, i.e. choke changed in its lifetime, it is not normally re-marked for the given choke indicated on the bores. If in doubt consult a gunsmith to measure the bore for you. In a side by side gun the right hand barrel has less choke than the left as standard. In the

The Countryman's Field Sports Bible

case of an over and under the bottom barrel has less choke than the top barrel.

Multi-Choke Guns

Multi-choke guns come with a set of screw in choke tubes and are marked as to what they are, and maybe worded as follows;

        True cyl   ¼ choke   ¾ choke

        Improved cyl   ½ choke   full choke

Or they may have notches or stars on ;

1. True cyl = worded
2. Improved cyl = 5 marks or worded
3. ¼ choke = 4 marks
4. ½ choke = 3 marks
5. ¾ choke = 2 marks
6. Full choke = 1 mark

Multi- choke guns are very versatile indeed for all shooting disciplines, whether game or clay shooting, one gun for all really. But of course chokes are only part of ballistics. One must use the correct size of shot to match the chosen choke for the quarry we are shooting and also the type of wad, whether plastic or fibre.

The Countryman's Field Sports Bible

The Wad

Ballistically, the plastic wad is more efficient than the fibre wad. It has a greater gas seal to the bore so the pressure within the cartridge is less, to obtain maximum velocity. This results in less recoil for a given load to the shooter. Also as the shot is encased within the cup of the wad, the shot will not come into contact with the bore, so less damage to the shot will occur and a more consistent pattern of shot will be achieved. One must remember though that a plastic wad throws a tighter pattern than a fibre wad; for a given choking, around 10% across the board in the following ballistic charts. But of course they are not very environmentally friendly around the shoot, taking years for the wad to rot down, also a possible hazard to livestock. So before going to a shoot, game or clays, always check which wads can be used.

The Countryman's Field Sports Bible

Diameter of Spread

Diameter in inches covered by the bulk of the charge of a cartridge at various ranges for all calibres according to the degree of choke of gun.

	Range in yards
Boring of gun	10 15 20 25 30 35 40
1. True cyl	20 26 32 38 44 51 58
2. Improved cyl	15 20 26 32 38 44 51
3. ¼ choke	13 18 23 29 35 41 48
4. ½ choke	12 16 21 26 32 38 45
5. ¾ choke	10 14 18 23 29 35 42
6. Full choke	9 12 16 21 27 33 40

The diameter of spread is interesting, let us take a look at the 40yd data. A good all round range sporting shot, one can see true cyl at 58" and full choke at 40" diameter. You may assume the true cyl choke at 58" diameter would give a greater chance of contact than the full choke at 40" diameter, allowing for human error. But using the same shot size in both chokes, remember the gaps in the shot pattern would be greater in true cyl than the full choke. For example; the target may not be hit by enough shot for a clean kill or may even fit between the shot pattern with no hit at all. The more you open up the choke the more shot or smaller size shot you need to fill the diameter of spread. Of course the smaller the shot the less foot lbs of striking energy is within the shot, so there is a balance of using the correct size of shot for the correct size of choke for a given

The Countryman's Field Sports Bible

target i.e. a small snipe to a goose. Before we look at the charts further, one must relate to the following:

Recommended Shot Sizes for Game
Shot Size

1. Snipe size 8
2. Woodcock size 7
3. Squirrel size 7
4. Partridge size 6
5. Grouse size 6
6. Pheasant size 6
7. Pigeon size 6
8. Rabbit size 5
9. Hare size 5
10. Teal size 5
11. Duck size 4
12. Geese size 3

Number of Pellets in Shot Load Game

Weight of shot   Size of Shot

	G	Oz	3	4	5	6	7	8
1.	42.5	1 ½	210	255	330	405	510	675
2.	36	1 ¼	175	213	275	338	425	562
3.	32	1 1/8	157	191	248	304	383	506
4.	30	1 1/16	149	181	234	287	361	478
5.	28.5	1	140	170	220	270	340	450

The Countryman's Field Sports Bible

Percentage of total pellets in a 30" circle

Boring of gun   Range in yards

1. True cyl   80 69 60 49 40 33 27 22
2. Improved cyl 92 82 72 60 50 41 33 27
3. ¼ choke   100 87 77 65 55 46 38 30
4. ½ choke   100 94 83 71 60 50 41 33
5. ¾ choke   100 100 91 77 65 55 46 37
6. Full choke   100 100 100 84 70 59 49 40

These two charts are a very useful guide combining the most common shot weights and shot sizes, also the percentage of total pellets thrown by a given choking at a given range. It is possible to calculate the number of pellets in a 30" circle for any of the above shot size and in any and in any of the six borings of the gun at the ranges stated by using the tables, number of pellets in shot load and the percentage of total pellets.

Example; shot weight charge 30 gram (1 1/16 Oz) no.6 shot, find pattern at 40 yds. Through a ½ choke barrel, total 287 multiplied by 60 from the percentage table and divided by 100 = Answer 172.

The 30" shot pattern circle is generally regarded as the kill diameter, and by shooting at a white washed pattern plate at a chosen range, say 40 yards, it will establish with a given shot size using a given choke, the gaps between the shot. Would the target fit between the shot, or not be hit by a sufficient amount of shot for a clean kill? This can easily be established at a clay shooting ground by offering up a clay pigeon against the shot pattern first on edge, this would simulate a (DTL) down the line going away bird or indeed a low incoming bird. If the clay fits easily between the shot then the choking used is too open for the shot size. Now place the clay flat on the shot pattern plate, obviously it offers a greater area for a hit on a driven overhead shot. So if you are shooting clays, multi-choke guns come into their own. Of course, do not go down the same road as

The Countryman's Field Sports Bible

many people, by blaming the choice of choke as their reason for missing a given shot, or change chokes at every stand thinking that it will improve one's aim.

Changing chokes must be linked to the shot size as well. Most clay shooters use 7 ½ for everything which can be a mistake. If shooting skeet, most of the targets are edge on and short range but of course, in the middle stands, if not shot in front, offer quite a long range shot on edge. So by looking at the percentage chart at 40 yards using true cyl i.e. skeet chokings, only gives you 40% of pellets in the 30" kill zone, which if using 7 ½ shot will result in "missed through the shot" pattern even though being on target. Watch the professional; you will notice if using skeet chokings, they always use 9 or even 10 shot to fill the kill zone to alleviate this.

Now to the other extreme, shooting DTL clays are a well out, fast going, on edge target that require a larger shot size with more striking energy to break the clay and of course a tight choke. So say a good shooter takes the bird early, at say 40 yards using full choke. 70% of pellets are in the 30" kill zone, using 7 shot which should result in a "no miss" even though on target.

Most sporting clays can be shot using ¼ and ¼ or ¼ and ½ chokings, using 8 shot as a good all rounder, and of course use the barrel select. Say on a pair of clays whereby the first bird is further than the second, shoot the ½ first.

So really you can see the golden rule, if you open up you must fill it up. Of course, as you will notice in the diameter of spread chart, never assume the greater the spread the more chance of a kill, even using a different shot size, as you will only be or get used to a diameter of spread if using

The Countryman's Field Sports Bible

the same chokings. For example; when teaching shooting for the absolute beginner I always used my golden rule, open up the choke and fill the pattern. This then enabled the novice a greater chance of a kill to start with of course, but over a period of time, once the target picture was in the brain, for eye to hand co-ordination, as any shooter should do, I started gradually to make the choke slightly tighter. This change would then make the student more precise in the placement of the circle of the shot pattern, so the better he or she shot the more I would tighten up the choke in relation to the hits. It is really like driving a car, the wider the road the more you use of it, with normally less concentration.

I learned this the hard way many years ago when shooting a fixed choke side by side, which I always do, which had ¾ and full choke barrels to which I shot all disciplines. It then occurred to me at the time to have the gun bored out to ½ to which I thought would take my scores over 90%. After a short time my scores actually reduced, partly missed through the pattern and also slightly poking at birds. One of the greatest clay shots, Percy Stanbury, used a side by side with full choke, as indeed some top shots of today, who seem to smoke the clays. Obviously I do not advocate this to the average shooter but from time to time most people drop in the scores and I do believe that we all may, with more open chokes become somewhat complacent in our shooting, relying on a greater spread of shot to cover up any human error. If you feel this is the case, tightening up your choking will force you to regain a more accurate placement of shot.

Chokings for Game

The Countryman's Field Sports Bible

This has always been a very controversial subject and of course before the multi-choke came into being, one had to have in mind when buying a gun what chokings to choose from. Most game guns would come normally quite open; improved cyl and ¼ was very popular and ¼ and ½ also. But of course, if using a fixed choke gun, one should consider the main type of shooting you will be doing before purchasing. Consult the following guidance.

Rough Shooting

Rough shooting is probably the most popular of all disciplines and one never knows for sure what type of quarry will present itself, but generally more choke is required in my opinion. ½ and ½ or ½ and ¾ would suite most targets, with a choice of no.6 shot or even no.5 for the larger game.

Pigeon Shooting over Decoys

Most of the shots offered will be over the decoys, so really 35 to 45 yard will be average range, ¼ and ¼ or ¼ and ½ would be a nice combination using no.6 or 7 shot.

Pigeon Shooting High Flying

This to me is probably the most testing of shots and very satisfying. Birds may present themselves 50 yards plus, so by using ¾ and full with 5 shot is ideal, the 5 shot carries well in the wind and also gives more striking energy than the 6 or 7.

Game Driven

So much can change in driven game shooting, basically by the location of the shoot. For most driven game traditionally cyl and ¼ would be advocated by gun makers using no.6 shot, but of course very high birds can be offered in certain parts of the country whereby it is not uncommon to use ¾ or full choke using 5 or sometimes 4 shot.

The Countryman's Field Sports Bible

Effective Range of Game Cartridges

It has been suggested that the requirements for a clean kill are;

SMALL BIRDS such as snipe = 2 pellets each having a striking energy of at least .5ft.lb

MEDIUM BIRDS such as grouse, pheasant, pigeon etc. 3 pellets each having a striking energy of at least .85ft.lb.

LARGE BIRDS such as geese, 4 pellets each having a striking energy of at least 1.5ft.lb.

If this is correct then there is an ideal shot size for each type of target, although the subject of shot sizes is controversial, the following table is a guide of effective range. It should be remembered however that many kills are made at longer ranges than those shown, but it is possible that they can be regarded as fluke shots, this is because some individual pellets retain sufficient energy to kill at ranges longer than those shown and although the chances of hitting are remote, if a vital spot is hit, one pellet, or in the case of larger targets, two pellets may be sufficient to obtain a clean kill.

MAXIMUM RANGE IN YARDS

Game	Shot size	Full Choke	Improved cyl	Mean for Borings

The Countryman's Field Sports Bible

1.	Snipe	8	46	37	42
2.	Woodcock	7	55	45	50
3.	Squirrel	7	50	40	45
4.	Partridge	6	52	42	47
5.	Grouse	6	52	42	47
6.	Pigeon	6	50	45	48
7.	Rabbit	5	52	40	46
8.	Teal	5	55	45	50
9.	Duck	4	54	46	50
10.	Geese	3	53	44	49

The Countryman's Field Sports Bible

Striking Velocity

The following charts are a good reference guide;

In feet per second at various ranges for standard game cartridges.

Size of shot	\	Range in yards					
		20	30	35	40	45	50
1.	3	915	804	753	704	657	612
2.	4	906	788	735	683	635	587
3.	5	893	768	711	656	604	555
4.	6	883	752	691	634	579	528
5.	7	871	731	667	606	549	496

Striking Energy

In foot-pounds for individual pellets at different distances for standard game cartridges.

Size of Shot		Range in yards					
		20	30	35	40	45	50
1.	3	5.79	4.48	3.92	3.43	2.99	2.59
2.	4	4.68	3.54	3.08	2.66	2.30	1.97
3.	5	3.52	2.60	2.23	1.90	1.61	1.36
4.	6	2.80	2.03	1.71	1.44	1.20	1.01
5.	7	2.16	1.52	1.27	1.06	0.86	0.70

The Countryman's Field Sports Bible

Details of Shot Sizes

			Weight per	Diameter	
Designation		Pellets 1oz 28.5	pellet grains	In"	mm
1.	LG	6	70.00	.360	9.14
2.	SG	8	54.70	.332	8.43
3.	Spec.SG	11	39.77	.298	7,57
4.	SSG	15	29.17	.269	6.83
5.	AAA	35	12.50	.203	5.16
6.	BB	70	6.25	.161	4,09
7.	1	100	4.38	.143	3.63
8.	3	140	3.12	.128	3.25
9.	4	170	2.57	.120	3.05
10.	5	230	1.99	.110	2.79
11.	6	270	1.62	.102	2.59
12.	7	340	1.29	.095	2.41
13.	8	450	.97	.087	2.21
14.	9	580	.75	.080	2.03

Relative Sizes of Shot

Pellets to 1oz or 28.5 grams

size	British	American	French	Italian	German	Belgian

The Countryman's Field Sports Bible

1.	1	100	72	74	79	75	104
2.	3	140	107	99	120	112	140
3.	4	170	134	113	175	140	172
4.	5	220	170	170	220	178	218
5.	6	270	220	221	270	231	270
6.	7	340	295	260	340	308	340
7.	8	450	404	402	450	422	450
8.	9	580	577	680	580	601	580

The Countryman's Field Sports Bible

Forward Allowance

The crossing shot whether game or clay, can be the shooters nightmare. Whether a slow or fast long shot, to a close crosser, we've all heard it in the clubhouse and said on the shoot. "I missed in front or behind." There are quite a few reasons to take into account for this.

Firstly gun mounting is an all important key factor in all targets, but in the case of a crosser one has to take into account the speed of the target and also the range. There are normally two styles of forward allowance, some shooters prefer maintained lead and others like the follow through type. Either way is still so dependant in the way we approach the shot. From the start, if at a clay ground, watch a shooter and on firing, notice from bang to hit, the time lapse and try to picture this in your mind.

But to regularly hit crossers, the secret is in the gun mount. Having the gun un-shouldered, first keep the muzzle upward to the oncoming bird, keep your eyes on the bird and start to shoulder the gun, keeping in pace with the target. You will now have the speed in the gun and also your body. Swing through from behind the target either in the maintained lead style or the follow through method. Ballistically, obviously the target is moving and during the appreciable interval of time that elapsed between the shooters decision to fire and the arrival of the shot charge at the target, and an allowance that varies greatly has to be made for this movement. The further away the target and therefore the longer the time interval, the wider the angle at which it is flying, the greater the allowance must be. It is also quite commonly supposed that a fast cartridge can so

The Countryman's Field Sports Bible

shorten this time interval as appreciably to affect the amount of time necessary.

This is a fallacy. For instance the time interval is composed of three periods. 1. From the brain's decision to fire to pulling the trigger. 2. From trigger pull to exit of the shot charge from the muzzle. 3. From exit at muzzle to arrival at target.

No.2 is very small and nearly a consistent interval, about one two hundredth of a second. The effect of the cartridge upon no.3 can also for practical purposes be ignored. This can be seen in the following chart where the difference in forward allowance between high velocity (1130 FPS) and standard velocity (1070 FPS) cartridges is a matter of a few inches only under conditions when the total allowance and the total spread of the charge are both matters of as many feet. There remains no.1 and this is the shooters personal time interval, this is by far the greatest of all the variants differing from shooter to shooter, from day to day and even from morning to afternoon. <u>The greatest variation in the time interval is produced by brain lag.</u> - the delay caused by the shooters personal time interval. However this may be overcome by swing, that is by shooting with a moving gun. If the shooter has learned to swing correctly, as described previously.

The Countryman's Field Sports Bible

The chart below shows the comparison of cartridges loaded with no.6 shot giving standard and high velocity.

Std. velocity 1070 FPS

Over 20 yard range	Range in yards
	30 35 40 45 50
1. Striking velocity FPS	752 691 634 579 528
2. Pellet energy ft.lb.	2.63 1.71 1.44 1.20 1.09
3. Forward allowance	5'6" 6'8" 8'0" 9'6" 11'1"

High velocity 1130 FPS

1. Striking velocity FPS	779 717 658 603 550
2. Pellet energy ft.lb.	2.18 1.85 1.56 1.31 1.09
3. Forward allowance	5'2" 6'5" 7'8" 9'0" 10'7"

The Countryman's Field Sports Bible

Weights of Game

Game varies in weight with the seasons, localities and age. The weights below may be taken as the average to be expected from adults in a normal season.

Blackcock 3-4 lb

Capercaillie 6-12 lb

Common Snipe 3 ½ -4 ½ oz

Golden Plover 7-9 oz

Grouse 1 ¼ 1 ½ lb

Hare 6 ½ - 7 lb

Mallard 2 ½ - 2 ¾ lb

Cock Partridge 13-15 oz

Hen Pheasant 2-2 ½ lb

Cock Pheasant 3-3 ½ lb

Ptarmigan 1-1 ½ lb

Quail 3-4 oz

Rabbit 2 ½ - 3 ½ lb

Teal 11-13 oz

Widgeon 1 ½ -2 lb

Woodcock 8-14 oz

Wood Pigeon 1- 1 ¼ lb

The Countryman's Field Sports Bible

British Game Shooting Seasons

Rabbits and Hare----------------------Not restricted

Red Grouse and Ptarmigan--------August 12th – December 10th

Partridge-------------------------------September 1st—February 1st

Pheasant-------------------------------October 1st—February 1st

Blackcock------------------------------August 20th—December 10th

Capercaillie---------------------------October 1st—January 31st

Common Snipe----------------------August 12th—January 31st

Woodcock (England & Wales)---October 1st—January 31st

Woodcock (Scotland)---------------September 1st—January 31st

Wild Duck and Geese (inland)---September---January 31st

Wild Duck and Geese (below the high water mark of spring tides) September 1st—February 20th

Coot, Moorhen and Golden Plover—September 1st—January 31st

Game shooting is prohibited in Scotland on Sundays and Christmas day, and certain specified areas of England and Wales on Sundays.

The Countryman's Field Sports Bible

Air Guns and Air Gun Shooting

Air guns have come a long way these days. My very first air gun was a 'Diana mixer 15' made by Millard Bros. Motherwell Scotland. It was in .177 calibre with a smooth bore barrel. Not very useful, but I shot my first woodpigeon with this gun using smooth bore slugs and it cost me 8 shillings and 6 pence, far inferior to modern day weapons. There is a very interesting story to this; after shooting my first woodpigeon with this gun my mother was not amused, for reasons which I did not understand at the time, and never will, and the gun was taken from me at 14 years old. "Never to be seen again, I thought," until 40 years later, something happened which I'll never forget.

After shooting my first woodpigeon, my mother gave the gun to Mr. Stonestreet our next door neighbour and told him to never to give the gun back to me. Unbeknown to me, after all these years he kept his word to my mother, until he died at 94 years old. When, after he died his son came into my gun shop and said to me "Do you recognise this gun?" I said that this was the first air gun I ever owned when I was young. To which he replied "This is your gun which your mother gave to my father never to be returned". He kept his word to the grave, and the gun still hangs on my wall at home today; this first gun led me to start a lifetime of air gun shooting sports and knowledge of air weapons of all kinds.

The Countryman's Field Sports Bible

Air guns have a very useful part in rabbit shooting - they are very cheap to use and run once purchased, and very quiet to use in good shooting situations:

There are 5 types of power systems which air rifles work on.

1. Spring powered weapons.

2. Gas CO2 weapons.

3. Pre-charged

4. Gas ray system.

5. Pump up types.

Which will be explained in the following chapters.

The Countryman's Field Sports Bible

Spring Powered Weapons

Spring powered guns have been in existence for a very long time now, going back many years. A few of the top manufacturers are BSA rifles and Webley & Scott, also the German Original & Anschutz, not excluding Weihrauch rifles and air arms, which have led to some of the very good spring powered rifles around today, which are very good weapons indeed. Air guns using the spring and piston are probably the all round gun for garden plinking i.e. fun shooting at cheap cost to the far superior hunting type weapon at full power which is needed for sporting purposes - however spring rifles can be used anywhere at any time not needing any gas or air bottles etc. so they are very versatile and you do not have more expense once purchased. Of course you do get recoil from a spring gun which may not be so accurate as a pre-charged weapon or gas type, but modern spring guns are very good indeed for most shooting sports.

CO2 Gas Weapons

It was, until recently that CO2 gas guns were on fire arms certificate only but now they can be purchased as per air gun law. i.e. classed as an air gun. CO2 gas guns have their benefits as they are recoiled, very light to carry in hunting situations, very cheap to buy, and very easy to use. Most Co2 gas guns rely on a throw away gas cartridge - their maximum power at the time of writing this is 11ft lbs of energy but this may vary from

The Countryman's Field Sports Bible

wintertime to summertime. The reason for this is that gas expands more in the summertime than in wintertime. If fitted with a silencer they are very quiet indeed as there is no spring or piston noise to contend with. On the whole CO2 gas guns are a very good all rounder for general pest control shooting. There are also very good multi-shot semi auto weapons for good plinking fun and many hours of good shooting can be had with this type of gun.

Pre-Charged Weapons

Pre-charged air guns are probably the Rolls-Royce of air gun shooting in modern years. They have transformed the face of the sport to the ultimate of precision shooting at the highest level of accuracy and are the most powerful air rifle you can buy. From the legal 12ft.lbs no licence required, to massive power outputs on FAC. i.e. Firearms Certificate rifles to licence holder only. There are many pre-charged guns on the market from all the top gun makers with a lot of different features, i.e. single shot bolt action which I prefer to multi-shot systems, bolt action rifles or various types of action loading. Pre-charged weapons rely on a power source i.e. a cylinder which can either be a part of the weapon or a screw on cylinder called a buddy bottle which is attached to the weapon. Either way the system remains the same.

Pre-charged rifles need a power source to pump the rifle up. This can be from a diver's air bottle or you can use a hand pump to fill the rifle. There are a few things to think about though i.e. where you live. If you buy an air bottle, which is easy to use, can you have it filled in your area, if not

The Countryman's Field Sports Bible

you may be better off with a hand pump, which is cheaper to buy and you do not have to rely on somewhere to fill your air bottle. All pre-charged air rifles are totally recoiled which is useful for ultimate accuracy and the trigger pulls are very clean and precise to use. The barrels on some makes are fitted with German Lothar Walther barrels, probably the best in the world, but on saying this all the top makes of pre-charged air rifles use very good barrels to match this type of weapon. All pre-charged air rifles come with a choice of single shot action or multi-shot type. I must admit I do favour the single bolt action type of loading, I feel it gives time to relax between shots and a more precise shot is achieved. Although shooting at night you may find having to load the single shot each time very cumbersome. i.e. lack of light to load.

Multi-shot weapons have a removable magazine or extra magazines which can be purchased. Once loaded it can be kept in your pocket and inserted into the weapon very easily. The shot amount varies from weapon to weapon dependant on the maker. Silencers or sound moderators work very well on pre-charged weapons as there are virtually no moving parts to the weapon, unlike a spring gun and are very quiet indeed. The ultimate in silent shooting situations. I do advise with pre-charged weapons that to get the ultimate performance and accuracy, to only use the advised shot count to every air fill of the weapon - it is very important to count the makers recommended amount of shots per fill of the weapon and count your pellets into a pouch etc. then you know how many shots you have fired and then re-fill the weapon with more air.

There are many top makes of pre-charged weapons on the U.K. market - you have probably the best range of choice and quality in the world from British air rifle makers. Choose a rifle that meets your needs and your pocket for the type of shooting you require. In all my years of air rifle shooting I can only say that the accuracy that can be achieved with this type of air rifle is absolutely amazing, and has brought air rifles into

The Countryman's Field Sports Bible

unbelievable excellence of power and quality which to me will never be bettered in my lifetime.

Gas Ram Air Rifles.

Gas ram type of air rifles rely on a strut very similar to a car boot lifter or piston type strut. This means that in place of a spring you have a strut which once compressed will take the place of a spring powered weapon. There are few advantages to the gas ram system i.e. they can be left cocked for longer periods of time - no damage to spring etc., if cocked for a long time and they are less noisy than a spring powered weapon. I also think a lot smoother to shoot and less recoil than the spring powered type of weapon, but you do not have a vast range of choice with this system of guns.

Theoben make first class guns using this system and also supply gas struts to convert some spring powered guns to gas ram. If you have a weapon that can be changed from spring to gas ram this may be a good idea for a long term project of shooting with this type of system. Theoben were the inventors of this type of system for air rifles and it is a very good way of rifle shooting if you do not want to get involved in pre-charged types of guns.

Please note:- the fitting of a .177 cal. strut in a .22 weapon will take the weapon over 12ft lbs - Legal limit. Weihrauch German makers use the Theoben gas ram system on some of their guns which are very good to use and will give many years of good service.

The Countryman's Field Sports Bible

Pump up Weapons.

Pump up air guns as the name suggests, are exactly that, the rifle is normally pumped up by the fore end of the gun using about 8 pumps for each shot, depending on the make of the rifle. I do not recommend this type of system for target or plinking i.e. garden shooting, as it can be very time consuming and a lot of effort. However these rifles can be very advantageous in sporting and shooting, being very powerful and recoilless. They are very accurate indeed, and when pumped up and loaded can be left pumped up for long period of time with no damage to the rifle, unlike the spring powered rifles. Also when fitted with a silencer they are extremely quiet.

There are a few classics of this type of air rifle which are no longer made and are very sought after by shooters who know what they want. Examples are the Sharp Inova or Benjamin Franklin made of brass of the highest quality throughout, also the Sharp Ace. If you can find a good example of these rifles, put them in your collection for sporting uses. I know they take a lot of beating. Look through air gun magazines or second hand shops, you never know what you will find. The classics are much sought after, but you can still buy a Sheridan .20 cal new pump up rifle which is very powerful and a good all rounder.

The Countryman's Field Sports Bible

CAL .177 .20 .22 .25

The calibre of air rifles has always been a very personal and controversial subject, which has been talked about and written about for years. I can give you over 45 years experience shooting with air rifles. There are four calibres of air rifles from which to choose, starting with the smallest .177 to the .20 cal then the .22 can followed by .25 cal.

Let us start with the .177 cal. which I recommend for sporting or very advanced target shooting. The .177 cal. is very fast to achieve the same ft.lbs. of energy on impact - this means that the lighter pellet weight will have to travel faster to achieve the same ft.lbs. of energy than that of a larger calibre to stay within the legal 12 ft.lbs. limit - also the faster you can get your pellet from A to B, the less drop of the pellet i.e. held over for longer ranges or under for closer targets. I would advise that for any 1 ft.lbs. limit air rifle to be in .177 cal. you will find that the very flat trajectory of this calibre will be advantageous to your accuracy. i.e. there is no point in having a cannon ball if u cannot hit the ship. It is very important to place your shot in the exact place of aim and the .177 cal. is my choice of calibre for sporting purposes or target work.

I personally own a Falcon pre-charged rifle in FAC .177 cal. with 18 ft.lbs. of energy, to my mind the ultimate recipe of superb accuracy and power. Very accurate at different distances of target, with type of calibre in .177. At this power I have head shot rabbits at 70 yards stone dead, sniping with a bipod rifle rest from a hide. A very effective way of shooting. In my gun shop 8 out of 10 will go for the .22 cal. Not for me, but people think

The Countryman's Field Sports Bible

the .22 is more powerful, not the case in 12 ft.lbs. legal limit weapons, they are the same in power but the .177 is more accurate at different ranges and easier to use.

The only trouble the .177 cal. has is its slight downfall in power over 18 to 20 ft.lbs. - this is about the maximum power you can get from the .177, meaning you just cannot get more air down the smaller barrel. However, as explained 18 to 20 ft.lbs. has a very flat trajectory from A to B and also good penetrating power at long ranges. A lot of people say the .22 has more shocking power, but to my mind I have to hit the target with precise accuracy - very important part in shooting, live quarry or target shooting for that matter.

The place of impact is very important in live quarry shooting - I recommend head shots for a clean humane kill, also very important when shooting indoors with .177 cal pre-charged rifle at 50 yards. I was able to keyhole shots off a bench rest, very reassuring when shooting live in the field. Also the .177 i.e. scope zeroed say at 30 yards will have very little drop out to 50 yards in FAC. very useful for all live shooting or serious long range target shooting. If shooting at night it is not always easy to judge different ranges so to my mind why make the task of shooting harder for yourself - but on saying this, if i could get a larger calibre shooting as fast as the .177 I would advise this, but in 12 ft.lbs. this is impossible to achieve.

The Countryman's Field Sports Bible

The .20 cal. slightly larger than .177 has always been a very 'not so very talked about' subject with rifle shooters. It is, however, a very interesting calibre for shooters to think about. Some people are put off by the lack of choice of pellet - or for that matter, makers of fine air guns - but the .20 cal. has a good following of shooters these days. It is a very interesting calibre to use and very accurate in 12 ft.lbs. or above in FAC types of air weapons. It has the flatter trajectory of the .22 at 12ft.lbs. With a heavier pellet than the .177 cal. Something you may want to consider.

In my mind the .20 cal. is a good all rounder for sporting uses for people that like to use something different and cannot make their mind up between the .177 or the .22 As i have said some people can be put off the .20 cal. by pellet choice, but these days you have very good types of pellets by top manufacturers on the market. Also these days most makers of fine air rifles use the .20 cal. in their range of weapons. The choice is yours to think about and you must be happy with your air rifle to be confident to shoot well.

The .22 cal. probably has a following of over 70% of shooters for many reasons. Most shooters assume that the .22 cal. is more powerful in the legal 12ft.lbs. legal limit than the .177., .20 cal. or .25 cal. This is a total myth. 12 ft.lbs. Legal limit power of air guns means the same in all classes of weapons i.e. they all deliver the same 1ft.lbs. of energy to the target, but there are benefits in all calibres whether .177, .20, .22 or .25 ballistically i.e. drop over distance. As I have said in 12ft.lbs. or below this velocity I would not advise the .22 cal. for many reasons to which many people will be confused but I will explain this.

The Countryman's Field Sports Bible

In 12ft.lbs. Legal maximum power the .22 velocity is slower than the .20 cal. or .177 cal. this means more pellet drop over longer ranges, making hold over or hold under the target more to judgement by the shooters. There is a simple rule of thumb. As soon as the pellet leaves the muzzle it starts to drop, so the faster you can get your pellet from muzzle to target the less time it has to drop. Example:- If you hold an object over a table i.e. a penny for example at 2" and drop it the amount of time it takes to hit the table is the time of drop. If you hold it at 4" that is the time of drop. Everything drops at the same speed, so now you can see the theory of speed of pellet from A to B. The faster you can get your pellet from A to B the less it will drop. Now you know the theory of velocity the .25 or .22 in 12ft.lbs. Is not recommended in my experience.

.22 and .25 Cal.

Some people think the .22 has more shocking power than the smaller cal. such as .177 or .20., but in 12ft.lbs. power the energy is the same at the target. Shocking power means nothing to me at the end of the day. I want to place my pellet where I want it to be delivered, at the point of aim, at different ranges. I know penetration at the target is more important than shocking power, especially in long range shooting. In weapons above 12ft.lbs. ballistics change again as I have said, I would choose .177 cal. up to 12ft.lbs. but over this the .22 cal. in FAC i.e. Firearms Certified Weapons, is a totally different weapon to use, to massive power outputs up to 30ft.lbs. or more. If you want to use an FAC air rifle up to this power then I would choose the .22 cal. or indeed on massive power outputs even the .25 has great stopping power in FAC rifles. Do not forget the theory of drop as in

12ft.lbs. rifles. If you want to use this calibre in FAC you will be amazed at its accuracy and stopping power.

The Countryman's Field Sports Bible

Air Gun Ballistics

Ballistics in air guns plays a very big part in successful shooting - probably more than any live round firing gun. Obviously firing a pellet by air to give consistent velocities was very hard to achieve by air gun manufacturers of yesteryear, in fact no old time spring gun in my opinion, gave great accuracy. They were using a leather piston washer with oil to keep it supple which would always diesel (the oil would vapour and basically explode on compression) and would give all manners of velocity. In fact most old air guns relied on dieseling to some degree to obtain their power output with very poor results in accuracy indeed. No wonder the air rifle of yesteryear is not considered by today's standards as the ultimate accurate powerful hunting weapon for small game, and of course field target sports. Most good makes of spring air guns now use a neoprene main piston washer with non dieseling lube to give consistent velocities.

As for pre-charged guns, most have air regulators built in to give the same air pressure shot for shot, but you will find pre-charged guns have a definite power curve, without air regulators. For Example:- on filling the rifle with air to the working pressure of your gun you will find using a chronograph, that the velocity is slightly less than say the 15th shot. Velocity will increase and stabilise itself, called the power band. It is within this power band you will find it more accurate; sometimes it pays to slightly under fill the gun for this reason. A chronograph is a must for air gun shooting in my opinion. In some cases you may find that a gun may creep over the 12ft.lbs. legal limit with use. It also gives you the ability to compare different brands of pellets to find the most compatible with your rifle, for the best consistency in velocity.

For an average velocity you just add five shots per brand in FPS (i.e. feet per second) together then divide by five. For instance, if your five shots with brand x pellets were 599FPS, 598FPS, 612FPS, 604FPS, and 606FPS

The Countryman's Field Sports Bible

they would total 3019 divided by 5 = 603.8FPS, which would be your average velocity. To measure the consistency over five shots it is calculated by simply taking away the lowest velocity achieved from the highest shot. Brand x registered 612FPS, and the lowest with the same brand is 598FPS, consistency is 14FPS - you are looking for the lowest figure possible.

To calculate average muzzle energy in foot/pounds you square the average velocity. Multiply by the pellet weight in grains using 603.8FPS as the average velocity and say, 14.5 grains as the brand x pellet weight, The calculation would be as follows:- 603.8 x 603.8 x 14.5 = 5286329.3 divided by 450240 = 11.74ft.lbs.

Now test for accuracy, you will be looking for the smallest group size. Using a bench rest shoot five pellets of the same brand at a 30 yard target to see which pellet group is best. What you are looking for is the pellet brand that has given you the best combination of accuracy and consistent velocity and power. (Within the 12ft.lbs. legal limit)

The Countryman's Field Sports Bible

Air Gun Ammunition

There are four main types of lead pellet, domehead or roundhead, pointed, wadcutters, and hollow points. Without doubt domeheads are by far the best choice for hunting. They have good ballistic properties and are more efficient than any other design at longer ranges, 35 yards and more. You only have to see any field target shooter, the most accurate users of sporting air rifles, and not one will be using anything other than domeheads. Wadcutters and hollow points are ideal for close range work to deliver maximum shock in mid power rated guns in and around farm buildings etc. Pointed pellets are probably the least accurate of them all, also it is a myth that they penetrate more easily. Take my advice and use a roundhead for all your shooting, close to long range hunting, as well as field target. As I have said earlier in the book, use .177 cal. for all your shooting, you will find it more accurate over different ranges and penetrates better at long ranges in the 12ft.lbs. legal limit guns. P.S. As I said before it's no good having a cannon ball if you can't hit the ship.

The Countryman's Field Sports Bible

Sniping Shooting with Air Guns.

Sniping shooting is totally different to walking around type shooting and is a very effective and enjoyable part of the sport. There are many different ways which you can adopt to have many hours of good sport. You now have a gun of your choice but you will need, for this type of shooting, a few accessories to go with it. SILENCERS OR SOUND MODERATORS are a must for this type of sport and there are many makes on the market, but most makers of good rifles supply one to fit and match the rifle. Silencers will give you a lot more shooting in the field. They work best on pre-charged types of rifles or indeed CO2 gas rifles, the reason being, you only have a release of air or CO2 gas, unlike spring powered type rifles that will have spring and piston noise. Although on these weapons you will still reduce muzzle noise and more down range silence. I have, many times when shooting, found that the quarry will not realise where you are when using a silencer, it seems to confuse your target. I remember once that I had three dead magpies on the ground at the same time, very rewarding.

BIPODS are a must for this type of sport - I would rather have one shot off a bipod than five standing up. Depending on the pocket, you can buy a cheap clip on one made of plastic, which is very handy to have with you, to one of the Harris type bipods. These bi-pods come with spring loaded legs to adjust height and fold back on the rifle when not in use, also you can have fixed or tilt types which fit on the rifle with a stud and can be removed very easily. Bi-pods really enhance your accuracy, and are

The Countryman's Field Sports Bible

essential for this type of shooting. I prefer the tilt type myself, it is a lot easier to use.

Bi-pods can be made easily for standing shots out of 1' by 1" wood. Simply drill a hole 3" down from the top and place some cord through, open out the legs for the desired height and place your rifle in the top. Very useful piece of kit and light to carry. HIDES are a must for this type of sport. I advise you to purchase a camouflage net of light weight type that fits in your pocket. This scrim type of net should be 6ft high and 12ft long. There are many colours to choose from to match all types of yearly seasons. A good all rounder is the ex-government type of camouflage netting, it is very cheap and will be of good service for most times of the year. Modern types of camouflage also come in advantageous 'timber' or 'real tree', very versatile types of camouflage to suit every time of year. You will also need some lightweight hide poles, adjustable in height. In most unnatural hide making 1 to 2 poles is enough. If you are sniping from a hedgerow etc. make a good hide and also use some natural local cover to blend in, always have spy holes to see

The Countryman's Field Sports Bible

through the net, you will not be seen as you have the hedge behind you as a backdrop. Never look over the net, always look through it.

The Countryman's Field Sports Bible

Pop up hides are a very useful shooting accessory to have nowadays, they are very light to carry and can be erected in minutes, or removed very quickly to a different part of the shoot, they also come in various colours of camouflage and can give you cover from the wind which is quite important if you are shooting for a few hours. These pop up hides have an opening door at the front so you can get very comfortable to shoot out. NATURAL HIDES can be very good if you have the right spot, say a ditch to shoot from or a hedge to cut into, you will need some tools though. A good folding saw is a must – very useful for hide building.

One of the best types of knife as I mentioned before is the French Opinel, it is very sharp and will give years of service. It is a very good idea to have

The Countryman's Field Sports Bible

a machete with you for hedge work, and a pair of pruning secateurs are a very useful piece of hide building kit as well.

Natural hides can be left after shooting to re-use with a little tidying up on each shooting trip and can be placed in parts of the shoot where your quarry will be.

Example of a natural hide (ideal for sniping)

The Countryman's Field Sports Bible

Crow Decoying

Decoys play a big part in sniping shooting and every decoy has its purpose and uses for different types of quarry. The Owl Decoy, either the little owl or the larger eagle owl can be used for crow shooting – reason being the crows will mob the owl in the daytime. The Owl Decoy can be set out from the hide, either on the ground or say on a fence for example.

When shooting crows it is extremely important to have a good hide and one must keep very still, the slightest movement and they will be off, not

The Countryman's Field Sports Bible

to return. It is a good idea to use a crow decoy with the owl. The crow decoy can be removed and replaced by your first dead crow. This can be set out near to the owl decoy. Push a small stick into the ground and then open the beak and push the stick down its throat – it will look very lifelike and when rigor mortis sets in it will become very stable. Be ready for the shot, you will only have one chance. Pick your moment for the shot.

Crow and Magpie Decoying

The strange thing about crow shooting is that the more you kill the more shooting you will have. What I have noticed over the years is that if you miss the crow it seems to warn off other crows either by calling or by wing beats as it flies away. They are not silly.

The Countryman's Field Sports Bible

A good crow call is recommended to attract the birds to get them excited and curious. Also my favourite trick to lure crows and magpies is to use a dead rabbit. Absolutely deadly – they cannot resist it. Set the rabbit out from the hide, it is a good idea to open up the guts a little and lay the rabbit on its side, the crow or magpie will come down to feed. I remember one morning using this system having three magpies dead on the ground at the same time. One shot after another and they didn't know what was going on. One morning I shot 22 magpies and 15 crows using the dead rabbit technique.

CROW AND MAGPIE DECOYING: I use a stuffed rabbit for this type of shooting and one can do this quite cheaply, with the advantage of going shooting when you like and not having to get a rabbit first. Sometimes it pays to put a crow or magpie decoy by the rabbit to attract, but always replace decoys with a dead bird as soon as you can, they work a lot better than a decoy.

Sometimes you will get more than one bird land, do not wait too long to shoot. Take the first bird and often the other birds will not understand what has happened and stay long enough for another shot. Very exciting.

The Countryman's Field Sports Bible

You can also buy Magpie calls for this purpose or an old trick is to use a matchbox with a few matches in and shake it, very realistic to Magpie calling. It is very important not to leave the hide to retrieve dead birds, only do this in a moment of lull. They will soon realise what is going on, they are very clever.

The Countryman's Field Sports Bible

RABBITS

The sniping shooting for rabbits is totally different again and good reconnaissance of your shoot is very important. You must know where pockets of rabbits will come out to feed as you cannot decoy rabbits. Once you know where they like to feed, for example; the corner of a field etc. build your hide in the hedgerow and let them come to you – that's what it's all about – summertime late afternoons or evenings are best. Do not leave the hide to collect dead rabbits until finished shooting and as I have said you will probably get crows and magpies coming in to eat the dead rabbits as a bonus. Also try to be downwind of your rabbits if you can and do not smoke.

If you find the grass too long to get a perfect shot i.e. cannot see the target clearly, make a squeak, nine times out of ten the rabbit will stand up on its haunches to have a look and this will enable you to take the perfect shot at a larger target. I will almost always go for the head if possible. If you miss you have not injured the rabbit. If you hit it, it is dead cleanly and humanely.

The Countryman's Field Sports Bible

You will find when doing this type of shooting that it pays not to shoot the same place too often for two reasons; one is you will soon eradicate the population in that area and two is the rabbits will soon learn danger. Try to have several sniping positions around your shoot. It is not a good idea to overshoot any part of your shoot too often. Rabbit shooting in the spring and summer play a big part in rabbit control. Every rabbit shot at this time of year is one less to breed again.

The Countryman's Field Sports Bible

Pigeon Decoying and Pigeon Shooting

There are various ways to shoot pigeons with an air rifle which requires certain knowledge and skill to have good sport. They are very wary of man and to come home with a bag full of pigeons is very satisfying, and can be very tasty for the table. Pigeons can be shot all year round and have no seasons like game shooting. There are different types of pigeons. The woodpigeon will be your main target in the countryside with a few collared doves around as well.

The Countryman's Field Sports Bible

Doves

Collared

The Countryman's Field Sports Bible

As with different types of pigeon, there are shooting techniques which are different for each species as they all have various habits and lifestyles which you can use to your advantage at certain times of the year. Pigeon shooting requires a bit more equipment than other types of shooting and it is very important to outwit these very wary birds.

RECONNAISANCE

In the countryside reconnaissance of bird activity is a must. Pigeons use flight lines and feed on certain crops at different times of the year. It is very important to see which part of the field the birds prefer to feed on or indeed which part of the wood they like to rest or roost in.

The Countryman's Field Sports Bible

Pigeon Decoying from a Hide and Equipment Needed

You have now done your homework, and you know in which part of the field the pigeons like to feed. We are shooting with an air rifle at targets on the ground, and this is different to shotgun shooting. First make a hide in a place of your choice with the wind coming from behind you. This is very important as the pigeons like to come into decoys facing the wind to land. Always put your hide up first and make it as comfortable as possible. Decoys should be placed out from the hide, 30 to 35 yards is ideal for this type of air gun shooting. Set the heads of the decoys generally into the wind, as pigeons never feed with their backs to the wind. You must make your decoy picture as realistic as possible for good results. Never put your decoys less than 3 feet apart from each other. You should have between 10 and 20 good pigeon decoys made of non shiny plastic. The shell type are very good as they stack in your bag and take up less room.

A moving decoy is ideal to use in the decoy picture. There are many types on the market from moving spring types to flappers and electric rotaries. Twenty nine years ago I invented the Marchant Mover decoy and have shot many thousands of woodpigeon using this device. The Marchant Mover is very simple to use as there are no cords or batteries to worry about and it moves and looks like a feeding pigeon. I recommend up to 5 of these decoys should be used to make your decoy picture come alive.

The Countryman's Field Sports Bible

A good idea is to have a crow decoy near your pigeon decoy picture. In my experience it gives the pigeons more confidence to come to the decoys and land. As said with air gun shooting you have to get the birds land in the decoy picture for the shot. Pigeons will usually fly over and around your

decoys, and if you have got it right, will land with confidence into the wind. Keep very still in the hide, movement is very critical. You will not generally have too long to take the shot as once landed they soon realise all is not well. It is a good idea to replace decoys with dead birds as you shoot them. Place the dead bird out with the decoys, push a small pricker stick into the ground, open the beak and push the stick down it's throat, then set the dead bird with its wings closed in the natural position. Always keep your decoy picture as good as possible i.e. natural – birds not set out correctly will warn others. You can shoot pigeons all year round and as the seasons change with different crops you can adjust your shooting accordingly. Pigeons have a vast choice of food, any sowed field of wheat, barley, peas, rape etc. can be a draw to the birds. Peas normally are a

The Countryman's Field Sports Bible

certain draw, they love them when they are sown and you can have a few weeks of good shooting up to sprouting time. They will even pull the seedling up to get the pea. After harvest time you will have good shooting again, pigeons will be attracted to any leftover peas in the stubble.

Pigeon Decoying – Crops

The same type of shooting can also be applied to wheat especially over wheat stubble or where patches of wheat have been flattened by the wind and rain in the summertime. Shooting over rape in the wintertime is also ideal especially in hard weather. A small amount of snow is what you want, once the rape has been cut good pigeon shooting will be had. The pigeons cannot resist the split rape seed and also the re-germination of the young seeds.

The Countryman's Field Sports Bible

ROOST SHOOTING

Roost shooting of pigeons is another aspect to the sport. Try to find a tree that stands out. a 'sitty' tree. Pigeons like to have an advantage point to roost in or let their food digest. A lofting pole decoy set works best for this type of shooting. There are some very good types available made of lightweight aluminium poles with a branch head at the top which holds another two pigeon decoys. You can use the telescopic lofting poles to place your decoys in the tree, 4 to 6 birds is ideal. Some decoys are especially designed for this type of work with hooks to hang on branches. Once you have lofted your decoys in the tree you can then place another 2 decoys on the branch head and loft them as well.

The Countryman's Field Sports Bible

Some types of lofting poles can have a fitment for a flapper decoy to be used as well. This adds a lot of realism to the lofted decoys. It is a good idea to use a small petrol funnel placed in the lofting pole to retrieve your decoys. It works very well and makes it easy. This type of roost shooting obviously works best when there are no leaves on the trees and your decoys will stand out very well. Make or use a natural hide in a position that gives you a good view of the tree. Afternoons till dusk are the best times of day to go for this type of shooting. Pigeons normally roost not too far from their chosen crop. Also look for droppings on the ground to indicate their favourite tree. In wintertime pigeons like ivy or holly and fir trees to roost in, also on higher ground, not in low lying woods which are too cold for them.

The Countryman's Field Sports Bible

Farm Buildings etc.

The shooting of feral pigeons around farm buildings or grain stores, barns etc. can be good sport and sometimes shooting permission can be obtained more easily for this type of shooting. Feral pigeon shooting will not incur so much equipment as woodpigeon shooting, as they are totally different to shoot. Feral pigeons unlike woodpigeons are more used to seeing and being around people. In barns at night a lamp is very useful for this type of shooting. The pigeons have all come home to roost and generally will stay put in the lamp for a good shot. This situation offers good sport and many pigeons can be cleared this way.

The Countryman's Field Sports Bible

Clothing

There is an enormous range of field sports clothing on the market these days to suit all weather and seasons of the year and all pockets. Basic camouflage wear is of the military army issue, D.P.M. which stands for disruptive pattern material. This type of camouflage wear can be purchased at reasonable cost from any surplus stores etc. I suppose most of us start in this way, it is very cheap and versatile and hard wearing. But clothing has moved on very quickly and a more modern outlook has been born to suit every situation. Advantage Timber, Real Tree and Wetlands and a host of others are on the market now, most are waterproof and silent to wear which is very important in hunting situations and a pattern can be had for all seasons of the year. It is very important in field sports to have lightweight clothing with plenty of arm room for shooting. One must have room in the elbows and shoulders to move easily. Gloves are important to the shooter, thin camouflage neoprene waterproof with trigger finger exposed are ideal. A good hat is a must for shooting especially in winter. A good proportion of body heat is lost from the head, and it can also take the glare from your face. Goretex wet weather wear is available in a host of colours. Goretex is 100% waterproof, breathable and very lightweight. Ex military Goretex is available in many camouflage patterns from any surplus stores and is very versatile in wet weather. The Gillie suit can be very advantageous for sniping shooting, although it may prove too hot to wear in the summer months, but overall it is an absolute must for any shooter. Never forget your feet, good warm socks and waterproof footwear. Whatever you wear in camouflage, remember it is movement that gives you away.

The Countryman's Field Sports Bible

SCOPES

There are many types of scopes available and sometimes the beginner is totally confused by all the pros and cons in various models I am sure. Really it depends on your type of shooting, whether hunting, field target or night time shooting etc. As a rule of thumb remember to keep the scope down as low as possible to the barrel, with the correct size of mount in height. For Example:- a 32ml lens use low, 40ml use medium, above 40ml use high, for 50ml and 56ml objective lens, and buy the best mounts you can to cancel scope creep. For Example; the lower the scope size the easier for 'hold under' and 'hold over' at different ranges than zero will be. The larger the lens size the more light can be transmitted into the scope i.e. dawn and dusk shooting.

Also remember that the more magnification you have on a scope, the darker the target becomes – again dawn and dusk. So in this instance a variable say, 3x9x40 gives you low magnification for dark and up to 9 magnification for daylight. A 40ml lens with good optics is quite good for light gathering, also a good all rounder for air guns up to 35 yards. Over 35 yards for hunting and field targets air gun shooting a variable, 6x24x50 magnification with parallax range focus and 'mil dot' reticule is very popular i.e. turning the parallax ring to focus the target the range will show in yards, this linked with the 'mil dot' reticule to aim the zero using the 'mil dots' to hold under and hold over. This is a guide to help you consider the basic pros and cons;- Try to buy a scope that your pocket can

The Countryman's Field Sports Bible

afford, but on saying that sometimes you may find a cheaper scope may have better optics with less features, which you don't want anyway.

For Example:- 4x32 or 4x40 will suit most air gunning target and hunting requirements up to 35 yards. Iluminated reticules are popular for low light conditions and normally can be adjusted to increase or decrease the level of intensity, but be aware that on some that the reticule or dot maybe too thick and covers over the point of aim. B.D.C. (Bullet Drop Compensation) Turrets are used mainly for target work which are marked for a given speed and pellet weight i.e. once you have the range this can be dialled in for a closer or further shot other than zero. My advice for a hunting scope is to keep it as simple as you can with good optics.

Mounting the scope properly is very important. Attach the mount on the gun first with the screws on the right hand side. Take off the top mount cradle and place the scope in, replace the cradle and screw up evenly on both sides just tight enough to allow to slide the scope backwards or forwards to give the right amount of eye relief i.e. seeing a nice round picture when shouldering the gun and also the cross hand dead vertical and horizontal. Then tighten down evenly obviously having the left and right turret on the right hand side.

The eye bell adjuster should be turned so that the crosshair becomes sharp and clear. Once adjusted, you will not have to do this again.

Zeroing.   Always choose a very still day to do this. It is quite amazing how the wind will affect left or right. Before zeroing turn both turrets in and out and to the middle, this seems to set the adjusters

inside better. I always zero an air rifle at 28 yards. At this distance it is easier to hold under the target before zero or hold over the ranges further than zero. It is very important to zero off a rest, most scopes move the

The Countryman's Field Sports Bible

point of aim. 1 click = ¼ " at 100 yards. So zeroing at 28 yards 4 clicks = ¼ " movement as a guide. Always fire five shots to see where the shot group is before zeroing, then adjust the scope to the point of aim. It is more important to have the left and right dead on as this will be the same at all distances. Fine adjust with one click at a time to shoot a good group of shots. Keep to the same pellets as described in ballistics. Pellets of different brands will not zero the same. Always use the same brand. Remember wind, always use a rest and take your time. Trigger pull is important too. Squeezing the trigger shot for shot. Breathing - When ready for the shot breathe in and hold. All these factors linked together will make you a more consistent shot.

Night Vision Scopes

Night vision scopes are a very useful addition to air gun shooting because of the range of shooting involved. i.e. 30 or 40 yards – the Generation 1 type of scope is adequate and can be purchased for around the £500 mark. Generation 2 and 3 which are in the 3K to 5K bracket allow for longer ranges and clarity. So really for the air gunner night vision can be affordable . Looking through a night vision scope is rather like looking through a green sweet paper with the live target showing up lighter, especially the eyes. The performance of generation 1 can be increased by an infra-red lamp which can be fitted to the scope. Some may have this built in, or you can buy an infra-red filter to fit your lamp. This will send out light, which is not visible, but the night vision scope will pick this up and will help to illuminate the target better. The reticule is normally a chevron but can have also my preferred cross hairs. Lasers can also be fitted and zeroed which when on target will really show up and make a good point of aim.

Night vision generation 1 cannot be used in the daytime at all and sunlight will damage the tube inside. Although most can be zeroed in daylight using a cover with a small pin hole in it. As with all things there are drawbacks. Night vision scopes have a different mounting system call "Weaver" so you will have to convert your mounting, which can be purchased, to use night vision. So having a rifle set up only for night vision is really the way to go. You will also find the eye relief is shorter so the mount must be able to be set further back than usual.

If this type of night vision scope is not practical for you, it is possible to convert your existing scope to night vision, by fitting a push on night vision unit onto the rear of your scope. These night vision units are cheaper to buy and are the way forward to only having one gun. They can be slipped on in minutes when dark. This type of push on night vision will only work if your existing scope has parallax adjustment. The eye relief will become very short and not always comfortable but if you can adapt to this it is not bad. Night vision adds a new dimension to night time shooting; to see but not be seen. Also if you lamp a shoot regularly the quarry can become lamp shy, so I think night vision is a very good way forward.

TIP: If the above is not for you and you prefer lamping, why not purchase a night monocular at around £100? This will enable you to see what is around before switching on the lamp. A very rewarding accessory to any lamping kit.

The Countryman's Field Sports Bible

Equipment in the Field

Mobile phones are a must really. You never know what may happen when out shooting, especially when out on your own and more so at night.

As I have mentioned before, I knew a man who broke his leg once and laid there all night in the cold, no mobile phones then. Always tell people where you are shooting and the time you are coming home.

TIP: Always take your phone but have it switched to silent. Sod's Law that it will ring at the time of a shot.

FIRST AID:

Always take a small first aid kit with you. Cuts and scratches can soon become septic after handling game, gutting etc and it takes up very little room in one's kit.

KNIVES: There is a large choice of knives for the shooter but first let us get the law straight.

The Countryman's Field Sports Bible

It is not against the law to carry a knife in a public place with a blade three inch or less with a fixed or folding blade. However flick, gravity, butterfly and some self openers including T Handles and T Handle skinners are illegal anywhere. Although a knife regardless of size may be purchased and also used on private land where you have permission to be.

Always make sure after the shoot to take it off your person. It can be all too easy to forget and go into a pub, shop or petrol station etc which would be a breach of the law.

Folding lock knives take some beating with a 3" or 2" blade for most skinning and gutting work. The French Opinel Lock No 6 or 8 is ideal. Made of carbon steel it really keeps its edge and cheap to buy and replace if lost etc.

Stainless steel blades are easy to sharpen as they are softer but of course do not have the long lasting edge of carbon.

Look for a knife with a lanyard fitting, very handy to let the knife drop whilst working with it, also cannot be lost. This is essential on an expensive knife otherwise you may just stick it in the ground and walk away.

Gut hook blades are useful for unzipping rabbits as the blunt side is against the guts. There is nothing worse than a cut gut to taint the meat. Knives are a very personal piece of kit. You will know when handling them

The Countryman's Field Sports Bible

which feels right for you. Knives will get covered in blood etc so look out for one that is easily washed.

SHARPENING

Always keep your knife very sharp. A blunt one is more dangerous.

There are many types of sharpeners available. Some require more skill than others. If you cannot keep the same angle and cannot find a diamond or wet stone to suit you buy a cheap ceramic rod (pull through type). Good for the job and anyone can use it well. Of course for the man who wants something different why not buy a knife making kit? Many types of blade blanks are to be had even Damascus steel and an array of handles, sheaths etc to choose from. It is not as hard as you may think and a great way to whittle away time making a knife to suit your taste.

EPILOGUE

I truly hope that you have found this book rewarding to read. I have spent my life outdoors experiencing the contents first hand.

Nature is the circle of life and if it is broken everything within it will suffer, including ourselves. Living off the land is a part of nature itself; everything relies on each other.

Enjoy your sport but always remember –

We have it in trust for those who come after us. It is not ours to dispose of as we please.

Good hunting.

The Outdoorsman.

The Countryman's Field Sports Bible

Notes

Made in the USA
Charleston, SC
19 November 2015